Collins

I0878598

Cambridge IGCSE™

Global Perspectives

STUDENT'S BOOK

Also for Cambridge O Level

Ana Carolina González,
Mike Gould, Barbara Miller
and Adrian Ravenscroft

William Collins' dream of knowledge for all began with the publication of his first book in 1819.

A self-educated mill worker, he not only enriched millions of lives, but also founded a flourishing publishing house. Today, staying true to this spirit, Collins books are packed with inspiration, innovation and practical expertise.

They place you at the centre of a world of possibility and give you exactly what you need to explore it.

Collins. Freedom to teach.

Published by Collins

An imprint of HarperCollins*Publishers*
The News Building, 1 London Bridge Street, London, SE1 9GF, UK

HarperCollins*Publishers*
Macken House, 39/40 Mayor Street Upper, Dublin 1, D01 C9W8, Ireland

Browse the complete Collins catalogue at
collins.co.uk

© HarperCollins*Publishers* Limited 2023

10 9 8 7 6 5 4 3 2

ISBN 978-0-00-854750-9

Endorsement indicates that a resource has passed Cambridge International's rigorous quality-assurance process and is suitable to support the delivery of a Cambridge International syllabus. However, endorsed resources are not the only suitable materials available to support teaching and learning, and are not essential to be used to achieve the qualification. Resource lists found on the Cambridge International website will include this resource and other endorsed resources. Any example answers to questions taken from past question papers, practice questions, accompanying marks and mark schemes included in this resource have been written by the authors and are for guidance only. They do not replicate examination papers. In examinations the way marks are awarded may be different. Any references to assessment and/or assessment preparation are the publisher's interpretation of the syllabus requirements. Examiners will not use endorsed resources as a source of material for any assessment set by Cambridge International. While the publishers have made every attempt to ensure that advice on the qualification and its assessment is accurate, the official syllabus, specimen assessment materials and any associated assessment guidance materials produced by the awarding body are the only authoritative source of information and should always be referred to for definitive guidance. Cambridge International recommends that teachers consider using a range of teaching and learning resources based on their own professional judgement of their students' needs. Cambridge International has not paid for the production of this resource, nor does Cambridge International receive any royalties from its sale. For more information about the endorsement process, please visit www.cambridgeinternational.org/endorsed-resources

Cambridge International copyright material in this publication is reproduced under licence and remains the intellectual property of Cambridge Assessment International Education.

Third-party websites and resources referred to in this publication have not been endorsed by Cambridge Assessment International Education.

All rights reserved. No part of this publication may be reproduced, stored in a retrieval system, or transmitted in any form by any means, electronic, mechanical, photocopying, recording or otherwise, without the prior written permission of the Publisher or a licence permitting restricted copying in the United Kingdom issued by the Copyright Licensing Agency Ltd, 5th Floor, Shackleton House, 4 Battle Bridge Lane, London SE1 2HX.

British Library Cataloguing-in-Publication Data

A catalogue record for this publication is available from the British Library.

Any external web links included in this book were checked at the time of publication, but the Publisher is not responsible for the content of external sites and cannot guarantee that links will continue to work or that the quality of the content has been maintained. The links are not intended to form part of the product and have been included purely for educational purposes. It is the user's responsibility to ensure the external websites meet their requirements.

Authors: Barbara Miller, Ana Carolina González, Mike Gould, Adrian Ravenscroft
Publisher: Elaine Higgleton
Product manager: Catherine Martin
Development editor: Judith Walters
Copyeditor: Catherine Dakin
Proofreader: Claire Throp
Cover designer: Gordon McGilp
Internal designer: Ken Vail Graphic Design
Typesetter: David Jimenez
Production controller: Lyndsey Rogers
Printed and bound by Ashford Colour Press Ltd

MIX
Paper | Supporting responsible forestry
FSC www.fsc.org FSC™ C007454

This book contains FSC™ certified paper and other controlled sources to ensure responsible forest management.

For more information visit: www.harpercollins.co.uk/green

Acknowledgements

We are grateful to the following teachers for providing feedback on the student's book as it was developed:

Mr Akash Raut, Principal of Firststeps IB World School, Chandigarh, India; Ms Shaheen Mohamed, Westcoast International Secondary School, Mauritius; Laura Perdomo, Anglo School, Uruguay

Contents

Introduction: How to use this book 5

Section 1: Introducing Global Perspectives 7

1.1 What's the issue? 8
1.2 Researching the issue 10
1.3 Planning a solution 12
1.4 Carrying out your activity and reflecting 14

Section 2: Developing key skills
Investigation 1: How sustainable is our food consumption? 17

This investigation introduces the concepts of issues and perspectives and the skills of reasoning, analysis and evaluation.

2.1.1 Analysing an issue 18
2.1.2 Analysing perspectives 22
2.1.3 Analysing arguments: reasoning 24
2.1.4 Evaluating arguments: expertise, bias and language use 28
2.1.5 Applying your skills 32

Investigation 2: Industry or tourism: which sector presents the best opportunities for sustainable development? 35

This investigation focuses on understanding research processes and strategies, and beginning to evaluate perspectives, sources and methods.

2.2.1 Developing research questions 36
2.2.2 Identifying perspectives in sources 38
2.2.3 Developing a research strategy 42
2.2.4 Analysing sources 46
2.2.5 Setting out courses of action 50
2.2.6 Conducting primary research 52
2.2.7 Applying your skills 54

Investigation 3: How can our team provide support for a local vulnerable group? 57

This investigation focuses on developing collaborative team working skills and written reflection.

2.3.1 Identifying an issue, points of view and teamwork 58
2.3.2 Researching an issue as a team 62
2.3.3 Deciding on and taking an action 66
2.3.4 Providing evidence of an action 70
2.3.5 Reflecting on teamwork 72
2.3.6 Applying what you have learned 75

Investigation 4: Should the global fashion industry change the way it operates? 79

This investigation focuses on developing independent learning skills, writing skills and referencing and citation.

2.4.1 Evaluating and recording sources 80
2.4.2 Generating ideas and structuring a response 84
2.4.3 Using sources and citing references in an argument 88
2.4.4 Applying what you have learned 92

Section 3: Developing skills for the written exam 97

3.0 Reading sources 98
3.1 Identifying and explaining information 104
3.2 Describing a perspective 108
3.3 Justifying opinions with reasoning and evidence 112
3.4 Investigating the strengths and weaknesses of research 116
3.5 Testing a claim 120
3.6 Evaluating arguments 124
3.7 Developing lines of reasoning to support a course of action 1 128
3.8 Developing lines of reasoning to support a course of action 2 132

Section 4: Writing an individual report 135

4.1 Exploring a topic, choosing an issue and formulating a research question 136
4.2 Identifying, analysing and engaging with perspectives 140
4.3 Analysing the issue and its causes and consequences 144
4.4 Researching different courses of action to help solve the issue 146
4.5 Making a plan for your essay 148
4.6 Writing an introduction 150
4.7 Discussing causes and consequences 152
4.8 Selecting perspectives and discussing them in your essay 156
4.9 Writing about evaluating sources 160
4.10 Making judgements about perspectives 162
4.11 Reflecting on your developing personal perspective 166
4.12 Making a case for a course of action 168
4.13 Writing a conclusion 172
4.14 Writing a bibliography for your report 174

Section 5: Carrying out a team project 179

5.1 Understanding the elements of a team-based project 180
5.2 Starting your explanation of research and planning 184
5.3 Honing your research 188
5.4 Deciding on an action and evidence 192
5.5 Planning how to evaluate your action 196
5.6 Collaborating to complete the project 198
5.7 Planning a reflective response 200
5.8 Summarising your research 202
5.9 Writing up your reflections 204

Glossary of key terms 209

Acknowledgements 212

Introduction: How to use this book

The Collins *Cambridge IGCSE™ Student's Book* offers a supportive introduction to Global Perspectives, with rich international texts, data and case studies to stimulate your thinking about contemporary global topics.

The book is organised into five sections.

Section 1 introduces the excitement of Global Perspectives, by asking you to jump straight into a collaborative project in which you research and come up with practical suggestions for how you can have a positive impact on an issue affecting students in your school. This project should give you a taster of the approaches and thinking processes that Global Perspectives involves, and it will allow you to reflect on the skills you need to develop throughout the course.

The four investigations in **Section 2** offer a deeper exploration of the skills and concepts that underpin Global Perspectives. Each investigation takes an active, meaningful, enquiry-based approach to an issue and asks you to apply the skills you have been learning to a final task. These tasks range from participating in a class debate; presenting a proposal to support a course of action; working as a team to plan and take an action to help with a local issue; to writing the opening of an essay on an issue you have researched yourself. If you are new to Global Perspectives, this section will help you build a strong foundation for the rest of the course.

In **Section 3**, you will analyse, evaluate and respond to two sets of given sources on two different topics. You will be asked to apply the skills and understanding you have been developing in Section 2 as you respond to a range of questions in different formats, to help you prepare for written examinations.

You will also read, assess and help to improve example answers to these practice questions. The answers have been written by our authors.

Section 4 will give you the opportunity to undertake a mini research project to help you understand the process of producing an Individual Report. The research process will be broken down into stages, with a clear focus on planning, structuring and writing a report effectively, and you will be able to share ideas with your peers and learn from some examples written by our authors. When you tackle your real Individual Report, you will need to work independently, and you will have to manage your own time to complete the report successfully. We hope the chapter will provide a useful reference point when you come to do this, and that you will be able to look back at the stages and activities outlined to help you manage the process.

Finally, in **Section 5**, you will be guided through the process of planning, carrying out and reflecting in writing on a Team Project, again looking at exemplar work written by our author team.

Throughout the book, examples of written work, planning formats and useful language structures for speaking and writing are included to help you reflect on and improve your own work.

We hope our skills-building approach will help you to feel confident about carrying out primary and secondary research, evaluating and analysing sources and issues, collaborating with others, communicating in different contexts and formats, and reflecting on your learning. We hope, too, that the contemporary global issues and sources you encounter in the book will inspire you to investigate other topics – exploring the global issues that are most important to you, your culture, your environment or the nation(s) to which you belong.

Ana Carolina González, Mike Gould, Barbara Miller, Adrian Ravenscroft

Key features of the Student's Book

The opening page of each chapter summarises the skills to be developed and issue(s) to be explored, as well as the final task.

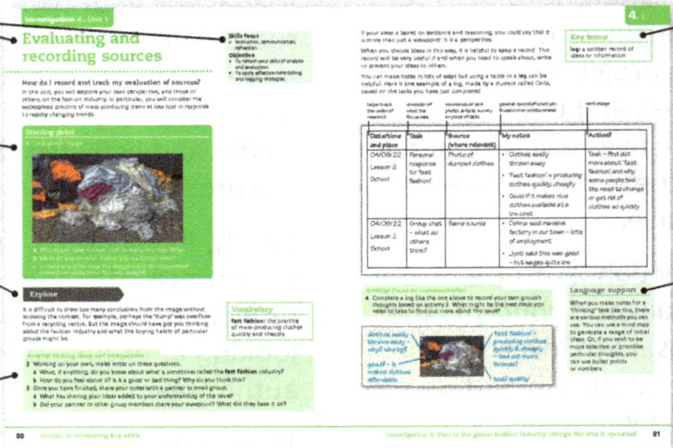

clearly demonstrates the focus of learning

short starter activity to get you thinking

activities build from supported tasks to more independent work

activities that build challenge across the unit

key Global Perspectives terminology is defined on the page and collated in a Glossary of key terms at the end of the book

offers useful phrases and structures for speaking or writing

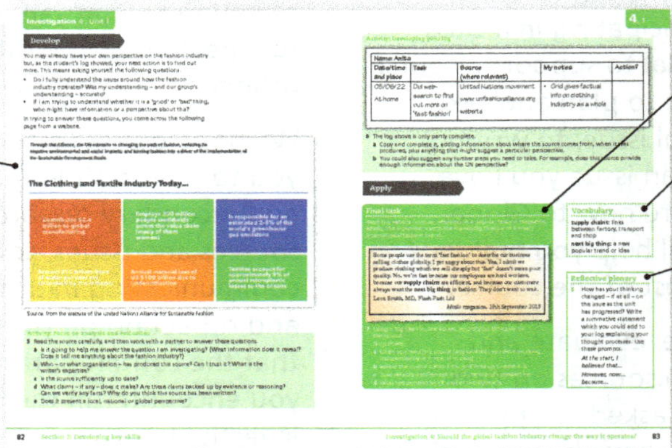

data sources, case studies and texts presenting different local, national and global perspectives to help you analyse an issue

Final task draws together the learning

Vocabulary boxes explain unfamiliar words and phrases from sources

Reflective plenary asks you to reflect on what you have learned, how you have learned it and how your own perspective has developed

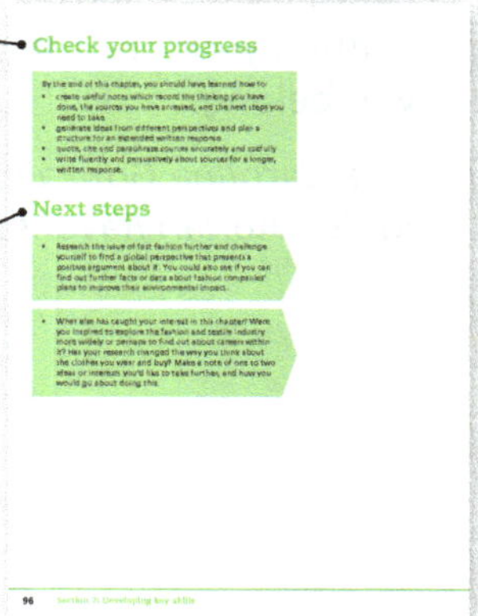

Check your progress checklist supports you to gauge your progress in the section or investigation

Next steps feature suggests follow-up activities you could do to extend your learning

Section 1: Introducing Global Perspectives

1

Investigation: How can we improve the health and wellbeing of students in our school?

Welcome to Global Perspectives. In this first section, you will learn how to work together as part of a team to make a difference on a global issue that is affecting students your age in your school community. This is because Global Perspectives is not just about gaining knowledge. It is also about taking action. It is time to carry out a project with your team and make an impact at your school.

The units in this section will focus on the following syllabus topic: 'Health and wellbeing'.

In your team, you will work collaboratively to identify an issue affecting the health and wellbeing of teenagers at your school and you will then do some research into the issue. You will use your findings to suggest possible ways to improve or help with the problem. Finally, you will reflect on the impact of your solution and on how you have worked together as a team.

In the investigation, you will focus on:

1.1 What's the issue?

1.2 Researching the issue

1.3 Planning a solution

1.4 Carrying out your activity and reflecting.

What's the issue?

Skills focus

✓ Analysis, reflection, communication

Objective

- To work in a team to identify issues affecting the wellbeing of students
- To begin to understand more about what might have caused these issues

What health and wellbeing issues are students facing nowadays?

The world we live in is characterised by rapid change. This presents a range of opportunities that were not available to previous generations. It also presents challenges that people in the past did not have to face. These challenges affect different people in different ways. Some of these challenges have an impact on the lives of younger people disproportionately. Sometimes it is necessary to target specific support for younger people.

In this unit, you will work as a team to identify an **issue** affecting younger people.

Key terms

issue: an important subject or problem for discussion

Explore

Activity: Identifying an issue

1 In groups, look at the images below and discuss what possible issues affecting students' wellbeing you can identify.

2 a Now, discuss with your team which issues you think are affecting young people's wellbeing in your school community. Agree on an issue that you think it would be important to focus on. (This does not need to be one of the issues shown above.)

Naya: An issue that affects our school community is the excessive use of smartphones. Wherever we look, there is always someone with a cell phone in their hands and this shows…

Ana María: You're right, Naya, but what about the lack of exercise? Now, young people love to play video games and…

b How is this issue affecting young people?

Activity: Developing a personal view on the issue

3 Now, in pairs answer the following questions.

a What might be the causes of the issue you are focusing on? For example:

> Everyone has a cell phone nowadays. If you're not online, you may miss out on something important.

> Content is so addictive that you just lose track of time.

b What have been the negative consequences, both at home and in school, of the issue? For example:

> Some of my friends don't exercise anymore.

> I also know that some people can't concentrate at school. They are just too tired.

c Are there any positive consequences of the issue? For example:

> Sure! I have learned new vocabulary while playing video games.

> Having a phone has helped me several times. I remember when…

Apply

Final task

4 Get together with your team and compare your answers.

a How similar or how different are your views on the issue?

b What possible actions could you take to prevent the causes from happening or to deal with the consequences of this issue?

Reflective plenary

5 Reflect on the following questions.

a What have you learned about the issue through your discussions?

b What additional information do you need to understand the issue better?

c Whose viewpoints do you need to understand the issue better?

Researching the issue

Skills focus
✓ Research, analysis, reflection, collaboration

Objective
- To learn how to research different points of view on the issue

Who can help me understand this issue?

In Unit 1.1, you and your team chose an issue affecting students' wellbeing to work on. You are now going to learn more by talking to people in your community who might have different points of view. Understanding different viewpoints will help you come up with a practical solution that meets everyone's needs.

Explore

Activity: Considering different perspectives

1 Consider the different individuals or groups at home or within your school community who could help you with your **research**. Complete the mind map below with ideas of your own.

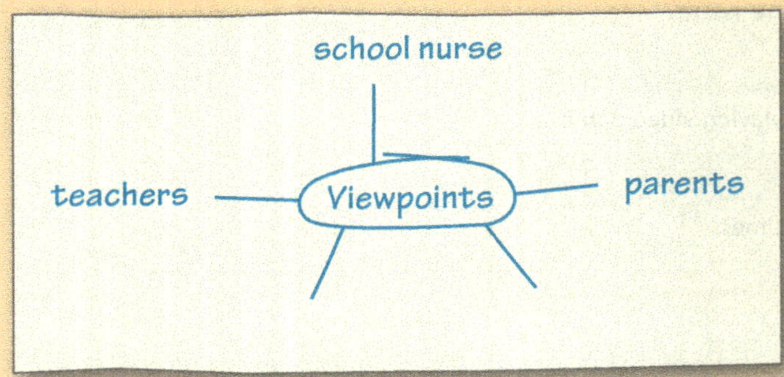

Key terms

research: the systematic study of a global issue to find evidence and develop understanding

Develop

One way of conducting research is to carry out interviews with the people you have identified. In order to write the questions that you are going to ask your interviewees, you will need to think about:

- the kind of information you are looking for
- who you will interview.

For example, students Fenhua and Hu want to find out different people's points of view on what causes excessive gaming; what people in their community think the consequences are; and what action people think might be effective to reduce the use of game consoles.

Fenhua: I think we should interview people and ask, 'Why do you think students play virtual sport instead of real sport?'

Hu: Right, and we could ask *parents* about their view of this. The parents will know how this affects their child, so we could ask, 'What are the effects of gaming on your teenager?' If they don't mention sport, we could ask them about that, too.

Notice that they avoid 'closed' yes/no questions at this stage. When they come to ask about possible solutions, Hu decides on an 'open' question first.

Hu:	We could ask teachers and students, 'What could be done to stop excessive gaming?', and then maybe we could test our suggestion by asking, 'Do you think a podcast would be a good way to inform students about excessive use of video games?'

Activity: Open and closed questions

2 Explain why Fenhua and Hu have decided to use open and closed questions to find out different things.

Fenhua and Hu presented their results in a short paragraph and drew up some conclusions.

> The school nurse gave us some really useful ideas about the chemical dopamine, which is released when you are gaming. It helps explain why students get hooked. Over half of the parents said their child's studies suffered as a result.

Apply

Final task

3 a Now it is your turn to conduct research. Use the suggestions below to help you think of questions to ask the people you plan to interview.

Can you tell me about your experience of students who…?
That sounds interesting. Could you tell me more about that?
What do you think causes this problem?
What are some of the effects of this issue at home/at school?
Are there any ways to deal with this issue?
Can you give me some more details…?

b Work in pairs to carry out your interview. Be sure to take notes.

4 Once you have completed your interviews, work with your group to discuss your findings, then summarise the following.

- What do people think causes this problem?
- What are the most serious effects of this issue at home/at school?
- What practical steps can you take to have a positive effect on this issue?

Tip: your practical steps can either seek to remove some of the causes or reduce or stop the consequences of the issue.

Reflective plenary

5 What do you think is an appropriate action to take on your issue?

6 How has your understanding of an appropriate action been shaped by the different viewpoints that you have researched?

Planning a solution

Skills focus
✓ Analysis, collaboration, reflection

Objective
- To learn how to plan a goal and choose an appropriate course of action

What can we do to help?

In this unit, you will plan a course of action to help make a difference to the issue you chose in Unit 1.1. You have found different viewpoints on the issue of student wellbeing. Now you will use this information to help you decide on an appropriate goal and an effective course of action to achieve it.

Explore

Activity: Setting our goal

1 Discuss with your group how you will complete the following sentences.

- **a** *The student welfare issue we are focusing on is…*
- **b** *This is an important issue because…*
- **c** *The aspect of this issue where we think we can make a difference is…*
- **d** *We are trying to influence…* (teachers, parents, students)
- **e** *We want to change…* (ideas, actions, behaviours)

Activity: Deciding *how* you can make a difference

2 Look at the word cloud on the right.
In your group, discuss the following.

- **a** How will you get your message across?
- **b** Why do you think this method will be effective?

course of action speech films
websites presentations teaching
documentaries outcome raise awareness
inform take action

Develop

Activity: Refining your goal

3 Now work in pairs to write your goal. You can use this frame.

> *Our goal is to persuade (who) ______________ to (reason) ______________. We will do this by (method) ______________. We think this method will be effective because ______________.*

Activity: Evaluating your goal

4 With your partner, you have just created some possible goals to help with the issue of your choice. Work in your team to decide which of your ideas is more effective.

- **a** Identify the strengths and limitations of each idea.
- **b** Decide which will be the most appropriate and effective one.

Amar and Sahil: Our goal is to raise awareness of the use of game consoles by teaching students about the causes and consequences of using them excessively.

Ganavi and Ju: We would also like to raise awareness on the issue but, to us, creating a website may be more effective because... Teaching, on the other hand, is difficult because...

the issue that they want to take action on

the message they want to get across

how they will get their message across

Apply

Final task

5 Now you have decided on the most appropriate goal, you need to plan how you will work together to achieve this goal. You will need to assign roles and tasks within the team and consider how long each task will take.

Use the table below to plan all the steps to achieve your goal.

Team plan

Topic	Students' wellbeing
Issue	
Goal	
Key action	
Team members	

Person responsible	Role	Task	Time required	Resources needed
Ju	Team leader	Lead group discussion to determine roles and task assignments	1 hour	Team project log

Reflective plenary

6 How would you complete these sentences?

You know you have got an effective plan of action when...

You can help to build an effective team by...

Carrying out your activity and reflecting

Skills focus

✓ Collaboration, communication, reflection

Objective

- To work collaboratively to achieve your project goal
- To reflect on your own experience of working as a team

What can we do to help improve the issue of students' health and wellbeing?

In the previous unit, you planned how to develop your project. Now, work together using your project plan to complete your goal. It is your chance to make a positive impact in your school community. Share your work with others and see how you can make a difference.

Explore

This is the course of action taken by the team looking at the use of game consoles. They have worked together to include useful information from the research to raise awareness of their issue.

Activity: Carrying out your action

1 Once you have done all your preparation, work together with your team to carry out the activity that you have planned to meet your goal. Remember to record evidence of what you are doing.

Activity: Showcasing your work

2 When you have completed your project, share it with others. You could:

- show photos
- present what you've done to the class or to another group.

Develop

In this section, you will learn how to reflect on your project and your activity.

Activity: Reflecting on your work

3 a Work with a partner who was part of your team. Together, reflect on what you have learned about teamwork and project planning.

Have a general discussion first, then use these sentence starters to make some notes.

- The issue that we chose was important to take action on because…
- The goal we set was…
- From the different viewpoints on the issue that we researched, we found out that…
- Our research findings suggested to us that it would be a good idea to…
- The course taken by our team consisted of…
- One positive outcome of the project was…
- This was achieved by…
- Another positive outcome was…
- This was a result of…
- An obstacle that we successfully overcame was…
- However… proved to be too difficult a challenge…
- This was due to…
- If we were to do this project again, one positive aspect we would repeat would be to…
- One way we could improve this project if we were to do it again, would be to…

b Compare your evaluation with other members of the team. What have your evaluations got in common? How do they differ? Has their analysis had an impact on your own evaluation of the project?

Apply

The game console team also reflected on the issue. They explained how their thoughts on the issue had developed, as well as how their behaviour or that of others changed as a result of the action they took.

Amar: After the research, I realised that I was being affected by this issue as well. I didn't know how much it was affecting my school performance and I am determined to control my use of the games console. I promised my parents and myself that I would only use it for one hour a day. This would allow me time to focus on schoolwork. I have seen the benefits of this change of habit and I can see the improvement in my school grades.

Final task

4 Individually, reflect on what you have learned about your issue.

a How far do you think other people's ideas have changed as a result of the action that your group took? Give examples.

b How has taking part in this project influenced the way you think about this issue?

Reflective plenary

5 a Think of an effective contribution that another member of your team made to the outcome of your project. What was the action? What was the impact? What enabled them to achieve this success?

b How could you adapt this approach to other situations in which a course of action might be needed?

Next steps

Now that you have conducted primary research about your issue, you can go on to research student wellbeing nationally and in other countries via a range of online sources.

You could find out what international organisations such as UNICEF suggest to improve young people's wellbeing and how international schools around the world are dealing with this. Finally, you could research how the wellbeing of teenagers will affect their adult lives.

Be proactive in researching global issues. Find out how they have an impact on your community. Listen to different people's ideas about what action should be taken on these issues. Think about how people express and provide evidence for their viewpoints. How effectively do they support their statements? What are their motives for getting involved with this issue? What practical steps are being put in place to make a difference? Are there any actions in progress that it would be worth supporting?

Next time you work as part of a team, at school or outside it, reflect on the challenges you have faced and how you overcame them. What do you notice about what characterises effective teams?

Section 2: Developing key skills

2.1 Investigation 1: How sustainable is our food consumption?

In this investigation, you will explore the issue of global food and water provision, by looking at sources and doing some research. You will consider your initial point of view, then look at the perspectives of different sources. Having considered the strength of the arguments presented in these sources, you will then reflect and come to a conclusion about your own perspective.

The investigation will focus on the following syllabus topic: Water, food and agriculture. During the investigation, you will also touch on 'Poverty and inequality'; 'Environment, pollution and conservation'; and 'Technology, industry and innovation'.

Your final task will be a class debate that draws together the skills and understanding you have developed to discuss this question: *Food and water: We should be able to have anything we want, whenever we want it. Do you agree?*

This investigation focuses on analysis, evaluation, reflection, collaboration and communication.

You will be developing the following skills:

1.1 Analysing an issue

1.2 Analysing perspectives

1.3 Analysing arguments: reasoning

1.4 Evaluating arguments: expertise, bias and language use

1.5 Applying your skills.

Analysing an issue

How can I reflect on and develop my personal viewpoint on an issue?

Skills focus
✓ Reflection, research, analysis

Objective
- To understand and identify issues
- To reflect on issues and develop your understanding of them

Starting point

1 In pairs, discuss the origins of the ingredients of your last meal.

Explore

What are the issues raised by your discussion?

As you reflected on your last meal, you probably began to identify that some ingredients were not locally produced. You may have wondered why it is an **issue** that the fruit you enjoy for breakfast comes from overseas. You may also have considered the issue of deforestation: of how the land now being farmed for crops to make biscuits used to be forest that fed wild animals and removed carbon from the atmosphere.

Thinking globally, air transport and shipping are used to carry ingredients all over the world. Why? This happens because some countries can produce foods that no other country can, and some can produce an ingredient more cheaply than others. Why does it matter? How and where food is produced links to issues of sustainability and poverty, and contributes to climate change.

How much do you know?

You are going to use an image as a prompt to start to think about issues around the sustainability of food production, its transport and consumption and to reflect on the importance of these issues nationally and globally. You will then carry out some research, accessing and interrogating data, to find out how far your understanding was correct.

Key terms

issue: an important subject or problem for discussion

Activity: Reacting to an image and activating your knowledge

2 The picture above shows the place where rainforest meets a palm oil plantation.

In pairs, discuss what you see in the picture, then answer the questions below.

- **a** What are your first thoughts when you study this picture?
- **b** Which do you think was there first, the palm oil plantation or the forest? What makes you think this?
- **c** Why do you think palm oil is farmed?
- **d** What foods are made using palm oil?
- **e** Which countries do you think produce palm oil?
- **f** How would you expect palm oil to be transported between continents?
- **g** Why might it matter that rainforest is destroyed so that palm oil can be produced?

3 How would you describe an issue raised by this picture and your discussion of it?

Your discussion so far has been based on your prior learning, as well as on your interpretation of the picture showing rainforest loss. The importance of this issue **globally** is well recognised, as it has an impact on climate change. However, less is generally known about the issue's **local** impact. It is time now for you to consider how you could find out about these local impacts.

Key terms

globally: relating to the whole world

local: relating to a particular area or neighbourhood

Activity: Research – developing your understanding of the issue

4 Work in a small group to complete the following.

- **a** List how and where you could find out about the local impact of rainforest loss. For example, you could use geography textbooks. What other sources can you think of?
- **b** If you are able to follow this up, find some of these sources of information and see what they tell you about local impacts of rainforest loss.
- **c** How has your understanding of issues around food production developed as a result of your discussion and research?

Develop

Activity: Interpreting a source image to provide more information on an issue

5 In pairs, discuss what you see in the picture above.

The picture shows land flooded in Bangladesh. It was rare for land to be flooded so badly before forests were cut down for farming. This source keeps our focus on the issue of rainforest destruction, while providing more information on its effects.

a What are your first thoughts when you study this picture?

b Does it seem better that the forest has been cleared for **subsistence farming** rather than for palm oil production? Explain your view.

c What do you think farmers are going to grow on this land?

d Do you think that farms such as this are owned by local farmers? Explain your view.

e What do you think links deforestation and coastal flooding?

Vocabulary

subsistence farming: farmers produce food to eat for themselves rather than sell

6 If you are able to, work in small groups to follow this discussion with some research. Each group should choose a part of the world where forests are being lost. Try to find answers to the following questions.

a Where is rainforest being cut down?

b Why is rainforest being cut down?

c What is being grown on this land, and where is the produce used?

d What is the link between cutting down trees and an increased risk of flooding?

You could share the continents of North America, South America, Europe and Asia between you. Keep notes of your answers and record which sources gave you the information you needed.

Apply

Final task

Reflecting on the global and local impacts of our food choices

7 Discuss your thoughts and research findings with your group, focusing on the following.

a Reflect on what you have all learned about our food choices and how they have an impact globally and locally. What issues have you found that relate to the demand for globally produced food?

b How easy was it to find the information that you needed?

c You're going to make a diagram using what you have learned. Start with something from a meal that you have eaten recently, that was not produced locally. Using the example below, identify local and global issues related to each item of food.

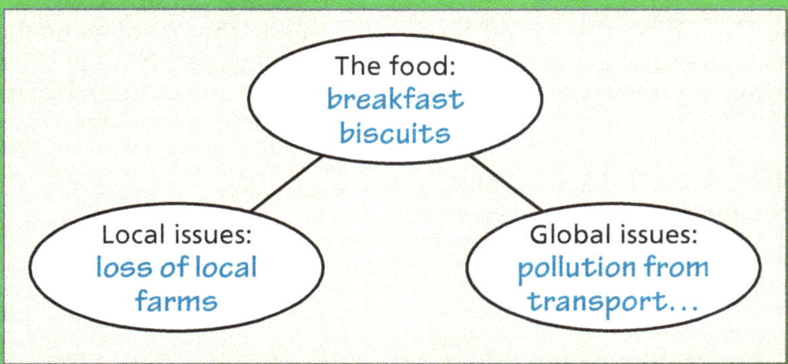

Reflective plenary

8 How could you find out more about this issue? In your group, suggest what international organisations you could research to understand more about the global effects of food production and distribution.

Analysing perspectives

What is a perspective?

Skills focus

✓ Analysis, evaluation, reflection

Objective

- To understand and empathise with perspectives

Key terms

perspectives: viewpoints on an issue based on **evidence** and **reasoning** (a **viewpoint** can be a way of looking at things for which no reasons are given)

evidence: information about a global issue that helps to develop understanding or prove that something is true or false

reasoning: thinking about something in a logical, coherent way

Starting point

1 In pairs, look carefully at the picture above and describe what you see. What might be happening? What issues does it make you think about?

Explore

As you look closely at the picture, you will become aware that this is no small local fishing boat – it is a trawler, used for deep-sea fishing. Trawlers can travel for months, taking thousands of tonnes of fish back to their home country, often for export. This is a huge industry. Ships work by **trawling** the depths of the sea, and some even drag their nets along the seabed. They are accused, by some, of doing damage to sea life and to the seabed.

You are going to look at a number of different interest groups and consider why they might hold different **perspectives** on the deep-sea fishing industry. The owners of the trawler will have a perspective as they own a business and believe it is their right to fish, for example.

Vocabulary

trawling: a method of fishing that involves pulling a fishing net through water behind one or more boats

Activity: Reflecting on an image

2 a The following groups might have a perspective on the issue of deep-sea fishing:

- the home nation of the trawler fleet
- businesses overseas that import the fish
- the Food and Agriculture Organisation of the United Nations.

Which other groups might have a perspective?

b In pairs, discuss *why* each of these groups might have a perspective. Note: you are not being asked here for the arguments they make to support their perspective, just why they might have one. For example:

- the home nation perspective → Why? Their citizens are carrying out a trade that creates wealth for families and brings in taxes for the government.

When you understand why a person or group holds a particular view, you have **empathy** for them.

Key terms

empathy: the ability to understand and share the feelings, thoughts or perspective of another person

Develop

This picture could be a market stall or supermarket shelf anywhere, selling fruit and vegetables from across the world. It raises the issue of the sustainability of food production. Can we continue to transport food around the world as we currently do, just because we *want*, rather than *need*, to eat it? What impact does this have on local food producers and on the environment?

Activity: Reflecting on a different image

3 In pairs, identify groups who might hold perspectives on whether we should continue to transport food around the world. Consider why the groups hold a perspective on this issue.

Apply

In order for a viewpoint to be classified as a perspective, it needs to be supported by both evidence and reasoning.

Final task

Reflecting on and developing personal perspectives

4 a What is your **personal perspective** on trawler fishing, and can you explain it? First prepare your ideas:

- Do you think it's good, or necessary? Does it need controlling?
- If it does harm, who or what does it harm? How?
- Who does it benefit?
- Do you have any evidence for this?
- Explain your ideas.

b Discuss in class and explain your viewpoint.

c Were you able to provide reasons and evidence for your point of view?

5 What is your personal perspective on the selling of imported fresh fruit and vegetables, and can you explain it?

Reflective plenary

Reflect on this question: *What makes it difficult to keep the good of the environment at the front of your mind?*

Key terms

personal perspective: an individual's response to an issue after learning, reflection and reasoning

Analysing arguments: reasoning

Skills focus
✓ Research, analysis, evaluation

Objective
- To identify and analyse arguments
- To reflect on the effectiveness of reasoning in arguments

How can I analyse the effectiveness of reasoning in arguments?

Starting point

1 In pairs, look carefully at this image. What sort of text is it? Where might you see it?

Vocabulary

authentic: genuine, real

In this unit, you're going to be looking at **arguments** and **reasoning**, and how they can be used to support **claims** or **perspectives**. You will evaluate arguments to see how strong they are and whether their claims are well supported.

Explore

An argument is a line of reasoning given to support or oppose a perspective or a claim. The reasons used can help to persuade others and guide them to reach a **conclusion**.

You're going to consider some arguments that consumers have made about visiting the shop selling authentic Greek food. All these consumers hold a perspective that importing foreign food is good, but for different reasons.

When you analyse their arguments, you're looking for **facts** or information that tell you whether a claim is **valid**. A strong argument will have its claims well-supported with sound reasons and/or evidence.

Key terms

argument: a series of statements containing reasons and evidence which support a claim about a global issue

reasoning: thinking about something in a logical, coherent way

claim: a statement or assertion about an issue

perspective: a viewpoint on an issue based on evidence and reasoning

conclusion: a judgement reached by reflection on arguments, reasoning and evidence

fact: something that is known or can be proved to be true

valid: based on sound reasoning

Activity: Analysing an argument

2 Read argument 1 below.

Argument 1

Julio

a Do you think that it is a strong argument? Discuss in pairs.

b The questions below help to effectively analyse the strengths of argument 1. Read the questions and the suggested answers. Then decide whether you think the claim is valid and based on a well-reasoned argument. Explain why.

- **i** What is the main claim in this argument? *I need to buy food from Greece*
- **ii** What reasons are given for the claim? *The shop is nice; I like the food; the flatbreads and cheeses taste better; it is imported from Greece; the owner is my brother*
- **iii** What is the problem with these reasons? What are the reasons based on? Is there any evidence? ***Opinion** and **value judgement** link the claim to the shop: the cheese tastes better than that from other shops; **Bias** or **vested interest**: the shop belongs to Julio's brother*
- **iv** What is wrong with the argument? *There are no explanations that are reasoned; who owns the shop has nothing to do with the claim; the cleanliness of the shop has nothing to do with the claim*
- **v** Does the argument make any sense? Is there any logic to it? *The reasons in the argument do not link to a need to buy food from Greece, so no*
- **vi** Would you say that there is any reasoning in this argument? *No, it sounds like a brother promoting the family shop*
- **vii** Is any evidence presented that supports this claim? *No*
- **viii** What is Julio's conclusion? *I sometimes buy from this shop that imports Greek food.*
- **ix** So, no, the claim is not valid.

Key terms

opinion: a view or judgement formed about something, not based on fact or knowledge

value judgement: an assessment of something as good or bad in terms of someone's standards or priorities

bias: unfairly prejudiced for or against something or someone

vested interest: a personal reason for involvement in an undertaking or a situation, especially expecting financial or some other gain

Develop

You should have a good idea now about what to look for in an argument and how to judge whether it is **valid**.

Key terms

valid: based on sound reasoning

Activity: Analysing an argument

3 Look at this example and see what you think about its validity. Work independently first, then discuss with a partner.

Argument 2

Ani

I need to buy food from Greece. My family moved here from Greece last year as I was transferred here to work. My children miss their home and life in Greece. They are finding it hard to settle into school and do not always sleep well. They are miserable and I am worried about them. Last month, I found out about this shop. I shop here sometimes now as it makes my children happy to eat food from home.

Analyse argument 2 using the same tests as for argument 1. Work with a partner to critically analyse the argument.

- **a** What is the claim?
- **b** What reasons are given for the claim?
- **c** Is there a problem with these reasons? What are the reasons based on? Is there any evidence?
- **d** Is there anything wrong with the argument?
- **e** Does the argument make any sense? Is there any logic to it?
- **f** Would you say that there is any reasoning in this argument?
- **g** Is any evidence presented that supports this claim?
- **h** Share your thoughts about whether you think this claim is valid.

Activity: Reflecting on factors that make an argument strong

4 What about this argument? Again, work with a partner to test the argument.

Argument 3

Ash

I need to buy food from Greece. All the magazines say that the Mediterranean diet is good for you. The healthy diet is about eating fish, vegetables and fruit, and the Greek shop sells some of these things. I love the amazing Greek cakes as well – sticky and full of honey. I really like them. I shop there sometimes as I can buy healthy foods from there.

a What is the claim?
b What reasons are given for the claim?
c What is the problem with these reasons? What are the reasons based on? Is there any evidence?
d What is wrong with the argument?
e Does the argument make any sense? Is there any logic to it?
f Would you say that there is any reasoning in this argument?
g Is any evidence presented that supports this claim?
h What are your thoughts about whether this claim is valid?

Apply

Final task

5 Work in a group. List the questions you would want to have answered before you believed an advert that said the following:

Reflective plenary

6 Work in a group. Create a spider diagram of questions that you think you should ask about an argument to decide its validity.

Save this diagram as you will be adding to it following the next unit of work.

Evaluating arguments: expertise, bias and language use

Skills focus

✓ Analysis, evaluation

Objective

- To evaluate arguments for bias, vested interest and personal authority
- To analyse the way language is used in arguments

How can I evaluate whether arguments can be trusted?

Starting point

1 In pairs, think of any advertisements that you find **unreliable**. Explain why.

How you react to an argument is influenced by what is said, who says it and the language they use to say it.

Key terms

unreliable: not to be trusted; untrustworthy

prediction: what someone thinks will happen in the future

verified: checked and shown as something that is true

Explore

Read the following source and the annotated comments. It is an interview with a scientist, Gabriella D'Cruz, whose work has been widely reported. Consider the effectiveness of her argument.

Vocabulary

bear the brunt: suffer the most as a result of something

mitigate: reduce the impact

Radio interview with Gabriella D'Cruz, a marine conservationist in Goa, who won an award for her work there.

How long have you had an interest in seaweed? "I have been studying coral reef ecosystems, seaweed forests and cetaceans for 10 years."

Why? "Seaweed grows close to the coast, so different communities here can access it without having to own boats. We have more than 145 species of seaweed in Goa. Coastal communities **bear the brunt** of declining fish stocks and are in need of alternative forms of income that are climate resistant. Seaweed is a promising industry that could offer coastal communities a stable source of income."

What can you make from seaweed? "Seaweed is a renewable source of food, and it can **mitigate** climate change – it absorbs huge amounts of carbon dioxide. Local people can also make businesses from seaweed that will bring them out of poverty. We have small communities making soaps and creams for tourists to buy. Other communities make seaweed into condiments to add flavour to the food local restaurants serve to visitors. These are small starts, but they are making a big difference to people's lives already."

Annotations:

a radio interview with this scientist suggests the work is considered important

*Gabriella D'Cruz's achievements as a scientist in this field can be **verified**, making her an expert with personal authority*

a fact that can be verified

strong or persuasive language

using the language of science to explain arguments

however, using facts that can be checked makes the prediction and opinion less of a risk in terms of truthfulness

*some **prediction** and some opinion here, both of which weaken the argument; these are not presented as fact, however*

opinion, but there is no sense of exaggeration, and there is logic behind this argument

fact that can be verified

Activity: Understanding the value of expert evidence

2 In pairs, answer these questions.

- **a** What can you see about the role of Gabriella D'Cruz that makes you want to believe her?
- **b** Her claim is that developing the use of seaweed is a good project from a local perspective. What arguments does she make about seaweed as a food that explains this?
- **c** She also claims that seaweed is good from a global perspective. What argument does she make that explains this?
- **d** Find examples of expert language. How does this contribute to her argument's strength?
- **e** Look at the language she uses. Give examples of words and phrases in the source that may lessen the value of the argument.

Activity: Expressing your evaluation in writing

3 How far does your evaluation convince you that the arguments about Gabriella D'Cruz's project are well made?

- **a** Make notes, then discuss with a partner. Note that 'How far' means that you should consider points for and against.
- **b** Using the information from activity 2, write a paragraph that weighs up the arguments.

Develop

Activity: Identifying weaknesses in an argument

4 Read the following argument from a wealthy man who lives on desert land and wants food to be grown there, rather than imported.

a Identify the flaws in his argument.

b Can you find examples of exaggeration?

c Does the wealthy man have a **vested interest** in food being grown in the desert? How does this knowledge affect your evaluation of his argument?

> Why should I have to buy lettuce and tomatoes from other countries? Using all that energy to carry food by plane or ship can only damage the environment, and, anyway, it means I can't eat what I want any time I feel like it. Scientists can put men on the Moon every day, with little effort, so surely they can put some of that effort in making such produce grow on my land.
>
> Why can't I eat food that I can grow right here, on my own land? It will taste better than anything I buy from abroad, so fresh and so amazing! I don't mind spending some of my money on this project. And I have been told that there is a grant that will help to pay for my land to have greenhouses where I can grow anything. I am so rich that I am bound to win this grant. Then I will be able to sell to others as well.
>
> This work would bring me so much pleasure, I can hardly dream of it.

Key terms

vested interest: a personal reason for involvement in an undertaking or a situation, especially expecting financial or some other gain

Apply

Read this extract from a charity website. It paints two very different pictures of life in one part of Africa.

www.charity ...

Makena, aged 5, drinks her tea. She then stands on tiptoe to get hold of the kettle hanging on the wall alongside the clean dishes. She has to hurry to join other children with containers of all sizes, and the group starts to walk more than 3 km to get the water their families depend on, digging it out of the riverbed. The round trip takes over three hours. The water isn't clean and sometimes children have to fight off the animals who want their share of it.

Almost 16 miles away, a 5-year-old boy, Absko, lives a very different life. He lives in an area where technology brings clean water. All the children in his village benefit from better health, better food and more time in school. This international charity took water from a mountain spring and piped it down to their community, using gravity to carry it in pipes to the village. Absko has to carry water to his home, but it takes only a few minutes.

Final task

5 With a partner, reflect on the importance of the work of this charity to:
   a the lives of those children
   b that African nation
   c our world.

6 You are going to write to the charity arguing that it should now spend money on connecting Makena's village to the same system.
   a Start by underlining evidence in the extract that will support your argument.
   b Now plan and write your answer.

Checklist for success

You should include:

- ✓ the course of action you are arguing for
- ✓ how this action will help children (think about the immediate changes it would make to children's lives, as well as the future impact)
- ✓ how this action would help the nation (again, think about immediate help, and also help for the future).

Remember to avoid using language that will lessen the impact of your argument.

Reflective plenary

As a group, add to the spider diagram you started in Unit 2.1.3. What else do you look for when judging the validity of an argument?

Applying your skills

How can I argue for a personal perspective?

Skills focus

✓ Research, analysis, evaluation, collaboration

Objective

- To reflect on perspectives and analyse arguments
- To work collaboratively to hold a debate

Starting point

1 Think for a moment what your own personal perspective on this question might be:
Food and water: we should be able to have what we want when we want it. Do you agree?

Explore

In this unit, you are going to draw on the skills and understanding that you have developed throughout this investigation to hold a debate on the question above.

Activity: Review learning, in preparation for a debate

2 You have worked with sources and your own research throughout this investigation.

a Work in pairs to complete the table below with arguments for or against.

Source	Yes, we should be able to have what we want	No, we should not be able to have what we want
Photo and own research: Palm oil plantation meets rainforest (2.1.1)	Transport means we can take cheap palm oil worldwide	Taking trees down to allow palm oil production damages the environment
Photo and own research: Flooding in Bangladesh (2.1.1)		
Photo and information: Trawling for fish (2.1.2)		
Various sources: The availability of imported food (2.1.3)		
Interview: New uses for seaweed in Goa (2.1.4)		
Water provision in parts of Africa (2.1.4)		
I want to eat fresh lettuce and tomatoes (2.1.4)		

b You will notice that each source can be used to support both Yes and No arguments. Read these different arguments, based on the first source. Then work independently to plan statements like these for the second source, to support each side of the argument. Discuss with a partner.

Alzena

Yes, of course we should be able to have foods containing palm oil. Palm oil is cheap for industries to buy and it makes really good cakes and biscuits. Transport in bulk by air means that transport costs are low. Why should we not be able to have foods containing palm oil, just because it means cutting down some trees?

No, of course we should not be able to use palm oil for our foods. If we want biscuits and cakes, we should have to buy only those that are made with local oils or animal fats. If these cakes and biscuits cost a bit more because the oils costs more, then we should be prepared to meet those costs. Nothing is worth the damage done to the environment by cutting down rainforests.

Amal

c Repeat this process for each of the other sources.

Activity: Choosing trustworthy sources and evidence

3 Now that you have identified your arguments, you need to check that your sources are trustworthy, that the arguments are sound and that the evidence is relevant. Then select which sources are useful. For example:

I don't think I would use the Greek shop owner's brother's argument to support my perspective, as he has a vested interest in the shop.

Develop

Activity: Collaborate to share knowledge and plan

4 Divide the class into two groups: one group will argue for the proposal and one group will argue against it.

- Bring together your arguments and plan each point.
- Agree who is going to make each point, starting with the strongest argument.
- List the likely arguments from the opposing group, and agree how you will counter them.

Apply

Final task

5 Hold the debate.

Food and water: we should be able to have what we want, when we want it. Do you agree?

Take a vote at the end. Which side won the debate?

Reflective plenary

How do you feel you did as a part of this team?

Check your progress

By the end of this chapter, you should have learned how to:

- identify and explain an issue
- understand and explain what a perspective is
- understand why people might hold different perspectives
- analyse the reasoning in arguments, reflecting on their effectiveness
- evaluate arguments for bias, vested interest and personal authority and analyse the way language is used to make an argument
- reflect on your own perspective and develop arguments to support it.

Next steps

- Research the sustainability issue with regard to food and water. What are the UN's sustainability targets for food and water?

- Find out what a range of food advertisements are saying about their products and sustainability. Select one manufactured food product and find out what is in it, and then find out where those ingredients come from.

- What else has caught your interest in this chapter? Were you inspired to explore the idea of sustainable food more widely, or perhaps find out about careers within food science or water charities? Or perhaps the idea of blogging or writing a personal article arguing a point of view is a skill you'd like to develop. Make a note of a few ideas you want to explore further about sustainability and the availability of food and water globally.

Section 2: Developing key skills

2.2 Investigation 2: Industry or tourism: which sector presents the best opportunities for sustainable development?

In this investigation, you will explore the issues of tourism, industry and sustainable development. You will consider different perspectives on how to develop a local economy, how best to conduct research, and what the best course of action to solve any problem might be. Your final task will be to present a proposal for promoting sustainable and inclusive growth for a rural area.

The investigation will focus on the following syllabus topics: 'Transport, travel and tourism' and 'Technology, industry and innovation'.

This investigation focuses on research, analysis, evaluation and communication.

You will be learning about or developing the following skills:

2.1 Developing research questions
2.2 Identifying perspectives in sources
2.3 Developing a research strategy
2.4 Analysing sources
2.5 Setting out courses of action
2.6 Conducting primary research
2.7 Applying your skills.

Developing research questions

Skills focus
✓ Research

Objective
- To recognise a good issue for research

What makes a good issue to research?

Starting point

1 When you investigate any topic, it is useful to think about what you know already.

a What do you know about tourism?

b What different groups of people are affected by this topic?

c Why might different people have different views?

Explore

There are different angles to explore any topic.

Rizwana has used six angles to organise her thoughts on the topic of Tourism and has created a mind map. For each angle, she has written down one thing that she knows and posed a question.

Activity: Generating questions

2 Work with a group to generate your own mind map, using the topic of Tourism and the same six 'angles'. What questions can you generate?

One useful way to see if a question is a good one to explore further is to see if you can think of opposing viewpoints or perspectives. Rizwana has researched the example below.

Question	Who makes money out of the online platforms where you can book holiday homes?
Viewpoint 1	The growing number of online platforms is good news for local people. This is because they can rent out their apartments to tourists.
Viewpoint 2	The growing number of online platforms is bad news for local people. This is because people from outside buy up apartments. This forces up the rent.

Activity: Identifying opposing viewpoints

3 Working with your group, choose another question from Rizwana's mind map above, or the mind map you created yourself. Can you identify opposing viewpoints for one of the questions?

Key terms

culture: activities such as the arts and philosophy that are important for the development of people's minds

politics: actions or activities concerned with achieving and using power in a country or society

ethics: moral values; the rules and principles that should govern human conduct

economy: money, industry and trade

environment: the natural world of land, sea, air, plants and animals

technology: scientific knowledge being used for practical purposes

Develop

There are other factors to consider when deciding if a question is a good one to explore. Rizwana has used this method to check her question.

Question	*Who makes money out of the online platforms where you can book holiday homes?*	
Will this question…	Score/points Yes = 2pts Not sure = 1pt No = 0pts	Comment
i let me focus on one issue?	*Yes = 2pts*	*Clear focus on an issue about tourism.*
ii be global?	*Not sure = 1pt*	*Are platforms global? What about where there is no internet?*
iii allow for different people's **viewpoints** to be considered?	*Yes = 2pts*	*landlords, renters, holiday makers, people who work in the hotel industry*
iv let me discuss **causes** and **consequences** of the issue?	*Yes = 2pts*	*Causes = demand from tourists. Better platforms online. Consequences = increasing supply. Rising rents for local people.*
v let me explore actions or solutions to resolve the issue?	*Yes = 2pts*	*Maybe better laws to protect renters?*
vi let me come to a clear conclusion?	*Not sure = 1pt*	*Could be complex. Different people could make money out of online platforms.*
Total	*10/12*	*Not a bad score. Maybe 'Should online platforms where you can book holiday homes be allowed?' would be clearer.*

Activity: Assessing questions

4 a Work in pairs to assess these possible questions, using the scoring system above.

- **i** Is it right to build hotels on farmland?
- **ii** What are 'cultural beliefs'?
- **iii** To what extent are the tourism and manufacturing industry issues for South Florida businesses significant and where do they have most impact?
- **iv** Can tourism support stable jobs?

b Which questions did you give high/low scores to? Explain why. Compare your answers with another pair.

Apply

Final task

Devising and checking questions

5 Work together to come up with high-scoring questions on the topic of Tourism. Explore the six different angles from activity 2. Swap results with a different pair and see if they agree.

Reflective plenary

6 Complete the following sentences:

- **a** *Good investigation questions always…*
- **b** *Good investigation questions never…*

Identifying perspectives in sources

Skills focus
✓ Analysis, evaluation

Objective
- To learn how to empathise with a range of perspectives

How can I understand why someone holds a perspective?

Starting point

Study the image below. Imagine you are conducting research in the community where this new development is taking place. You ask different people the survey question on the right.

1 What reasons might people give you for their different views? Make some notes and discuss your ideas with a partner.

Give your opinion of the statement: 'This development will benefit me personally.'

- Strongly Agree ☐
- Agree ☐
- Undecided ☐
- Disagree ☐
- Strongly Disagree ☐

Explain your view.

Explore

The term **empathy** usually means being able to understand and share another person's feelings and emotions. In Global Perspectives, the word takes on a slightly different meaning. It refers to the skill of understanding someone else's perspective. Empathising with another perspective does not mean that you have to agree with it. It does mean considering carefully the reasons behind the argument and the **context** in which it is made.

Key terms

empathy: the ability to understand someone else's perspective

context: the context of an idea or event is the general situation that relates to it, and which helps it to be understood

case study: gives specific information about something or someone and their development over a period of time; case studies are often chosen by researchers because the particular case represents a wider phenomenon

viewpoint: someone's viewpoint on an issue is the way that they think about it; for example, they might agree or disagree with something; a viewpoint may or may not be supported by evidence/reasoning

perspective: a viewpoint on an issue based on evidence and reasoning

Irfan is a student who has been researching the issue of tourism by looking at a **case study** of a new tourist complex under construction. He has found one blog and one news report that quote contrasting **viewpoints** from different **perspectives** on the issue.

Aida Miguelena, leader of Community Council

Manuel Arias, director of Regal Holidays

Extract from source A

'This is devastating for our community. Many will just leave,' said Aida Miguelena, leader of the coastal town of Tupillo's Community Council. 'Our survey shows that the vast majority of residents value tranquillity and natural beauty. They want to maintain the way of life they love.

Now our beach is jammed with construction vehicles. The area inland is being entirely stripped of vegetation. This development must be stopped.

We are heartbroken by the destruction but not surprised. The track record of this company shows that they always put profits before people.'

Extract from source B

Manuel Arias, director of Regal Holidays, said the complex is designed to accommodate 4,500 visitors and will create up to 3,000 urgently needed jobs.

'The tourism sector has already proved its potential by providing 10% of our **GDP**. This $500 million complex must be completed to provide the kickstart our country's economy needs.'

Mr Arias said that environmental concerns have been overstated. 'We commissioned a full impact assessment which has been submitted to the ministry,' he added. 'It clearly sets out how we will replace all forest and coral removed.'

Activity: Classifying perspectives

2 Work with a partner.

- **a** Which extract offers a positive viewpoint on the **issue**?
- **b** Which extract offers a negative viewpoint?

Vocabulary

GDP: a country's Gross Domestic Product is the total value of all the goods it has produced and the services it has provided in a particular year, not including its income from investments in other countries

Key terms

issue: an important subject or problem for discussion

Develop

Irfan has analysed Aida Miguelena's perspective, by adding his own annotations on the text.

'This is devastating for our community. Many will just leave,' said Aida Miguelena, leader of the coastal town of Tupillo's Community Council. 'Our survey shows that the vast majority of residents value tranquillity and natural beauty. They want to maintain the way of life they love.

Now our beach is jammed with construction vehicles. The area inland is being entirely stripped of vegetation. This development must be stopped.'

her viewpoint — 'This is devastating for our community.

claim — Many will just leave

reasoning behind her viewpoint — 'Our survey shows that the vast majority of residents value tranquillity and natural beauty. They want to maintain the way of life they love.

consequences — Now our beach is jammed with construction vehicles. The area inland is being entirely stripped of vegetation.

suggested action — This development must be stopped.'

Activity: Analysing perspectives

3 Now work with your partner to analyse Manuel Arias's perspective.
   a Describe the issue that he identifies.
   b According to him, what **causes** this issue to be important?
   c What are the **consequences** of the issue?
   d What claims does he make?
   e Does he offer evidence and/or reasoning to support these claims?
   f What action does he suggest?

Key terms

claim: a statement or assertion about an issue

causes: responsible for making something happen

consequences: results or effects of something

Here is another perspective on the issue of tourism.

Dear Editor,

Your travel correspondent [Gazette 15 04 22] is guilty of distortion. The aviation industry has a massive impact on global CO_2 emissions. According to the Sustainable Travel website, 8% of the world's carbon emissions are caused by tourism, and transport makes up half of that total. Tourist flights will have a major impact on whether the goals of the Paris Agreement are met or not. Meeting emissions targets requires government action. Effective actions by governments across the globe have one factor in common – the use of taxation that will keep the cost of travel high, and therefore help control passenger numbers. A global minimum level of air tax is needed now to ensure a level playing field between countries.

Yours etc.

Fatima Ahmed

Activity: Analysing a source

4 Work independently to answer these questions.

- **a** Describe the issue that Fatima Ahmed identifies.
- **b** According to Fatima, what causes this issue to be important?
- **c** What are the consequences of the issue?
- **d** What claims does she make?
- **e** Does she offer evidence and/or reasoning to support these claims?
- **f** What action or solution does she suggest?

Apply

Final task

5 You are going to be developing a perspective on an aspect of the issue of tourism.

Select an angle on the issue that you would like to explore further: for example, economics, politics or the environment.

You could choose to work with others who share a similar interest.

- **a** Select your angle, using the mind map on page 36 for ideas.
- **b** Agree a research question as a focus. Use the grid on page 37 to check that it is an appropriate question for investigating different perspectives.
- **c** Who would be affected by this issue? Make a list.
- **d** Think of two possible contrasting viewpoints that people could have on this issue. Write one sentence for each.
- **e** Think of some reasoning/evidence that could be used in support of each viewpoint. This viewpoint is now a perspective.
- **f** Write one short paragraph to set out each perspective. Use the sentences you came up with in **d)** to start your paragraphs.

Challenge: Try to match some of the people that you identified in **c** with the perspective that they would be most likely to agree with.

Reflective plenary

6 What is the difference between empathising with a perspective and agreeing with it? Be ready to share your ideas in a discussion.

Developing a research strategy

Skills focus
✓ Research, evaluation

Objective
- To learn how to assess the strengths and limitations of a research strategy

How can I assess the strengths and limitations of a research strategy?

Starting point

'Current levels of international tourism are **sustainable**.'

1 How could you find out if this statement is true? What facts would be useful to know? Where could you find them? Whose perspectives would be useful? Could any useful information be obtained at first hand – i.e. by using **primary research** methods?

a Record your ideas in a table like the one below.

	Suggestions	Where I could find them
What facts would be useful to know?		
Whose perspectives would be useful?		

b Compare your ideas with a partner.

Vocabulary

sustainable: the use of natural resources at a level that is not likely to damage the environment

Explore

In this section, you will learn how to come up with an effective research strategy.

Effective research strategies help you to:

- explore the causes and consequences of your chosen global issue with greater clarity
- suggest appropriate **course(s) of action** with greater precision.

Nadia and Kasim are discussing how they could test the claim that current levels of international tourism are sustainable.

Key terms

primary research: obtaining information that has not been available before; strategies include interviews and questionnaires – observation is another possibility

course of action: an action or solution to an issue or problem

Nadia:	It would be good to check out travel industry magazines. We could read interviews with travel industry leaders. They have direct experience of the sector.
Kasim:	That's true but industry representatives have a vested interest in presenting the sector positively. What could cause the industry to be more sustainable, do you think?
Nadia:	The fuel consumption of passenger aircraft is something that can be measured **objectively**. Internet searches allow you to cross check.
Kasim:	I agree. I would like to look at some literature produced by an organisation that campaigns on environmental issues.
Nadia:	But wouldn't they be **biased** against the people who work in the aircraft industry?
Kasim:	I still think it is an important perspective. They might put forward solutions to the issue.
Nadia:	I looked up 'future plans sustainability' and the name of an aircraft company. The results were immediate but there were over six million! Which to choose?
Kasim:	That tells you what *could* happen in the future. It doesn't tell you what the situation is now. It doesn't tell you if the situation now is better than it used to be. Things could be getting worse.
Nadia:	You have got to ask too why that information was produced. It could be classed as company **spin**.
Kasim:	What do you think about primary research?
Nadia:	It could give us a local perspective.
Kasim:	What, like interviews? Time-consuming!
Nadia:	But we might be able to find out if or how local people consider sustainability when they make travel plans. We wouldn't find that online easily – or in the library.

Key terms

objectively: in a way that is not influenced by personal feelings or opinions

biased: unfairly prejudiced for or against something or someone

Vocabulary

spin: when information or an event is presented in a particular way in order to encourage people to view it more positively

Activity: Sources of information

2 What sources of information do Nadia and Kasim discuss? What advantages and limitations do they identify? Discuss with a partner and record your findings in a table like the one below. The first one has been done for you.

Source of information	Advantages	Limitations
travel industry magazines, interviews with industry leaders	*direct experience of the sector*	*a vested interest in presenting the sector positively*

Develop

Activity: Evaluating sources

3 Work in groups.

a Share the sources of information and perspectives that you suggested in activity 1. If you can, take time to locate some of these.

Discuss their advantages and disadvantages using these questions to test a source's relevance and credibility:

i Is it going to help answer my question?

ii Is it sufficiently up to date?

iii What is the writer's expertise?

iv What claims does it make and are the claims backed up with evidence/reasoning?

v Can we verify the facts?

vi Why was this source written?

b Record your evaluation in a table like the one below.

Source of information	Advantages	Limitations

Activity: Using social media platforms

4 Imagine that Nadia and Kasim find a series of short videos uploaded by a young woman to a social media platform. In the videos, she gives her perspective on her experience of travelling from her home city to popular tourist destinations without using air travel. Discuss with a friend:

a Would you use the same criteria as in Activity **3a** to evaluate this source?

b Is there anything particular about using content from a social media platform that you would need to be careful about?

Apply

Final task

5 'The manufacturing industry creates far less pollution now than it did 30 years ago.'

a How could you find out if this statement is true? What facts would be useful to know? Where could you find them? Whose perspectives would be useful? Make a list of **secondary sources**.

b Could any useful information be obtained by using primary research methods? Make a separate list.

c Discuss the advantages and disadvantages of the sources of information that you have identified. Use the questions from activity 3 to help you.

d Record your evaluation in a table like you did in activity 2 and 3. Be ready to present some of your evaluations to the class.

Reflective plenary

6 If someone two years younger than you asked how they could assess the strengths and limitations of a research strategy, how would you explain it to them?

Complete these sentences.

You should try to… because…

You should avoid… because…

Key terms

secondary sources: information that comes from research already conducted and published by other people

Analysing sources

When I have found a good source, what do I do with it?

Skills focus
✓ Analysis, evaluation

Objective
- To learn how to interpret and analyse a source

Starting point

1 Think of a situation when you have had to make a choice. This could be, for example, choosing which subject to study further at school or something as simple as choosing what route to take for a journey. Make notes to answer the following questions and compare your answers with a partner.

a Think of a source of information that enabled you to make an informed decision.

b Identify the information from that source that you found most useful.

c Explain how that information influenced your final decision.

Explore

In the previous unit, you considered how to decide whether or not a source was useful to an enquiry. In this unit, you will focus on what to do once you have identified a source that is useful. You will explore some strategies for gaining meaning from both written perspectives and statistics.

Afua and Kwame have been investigating whether tourism or the manufacturing industry represents the better course for sustainable development. They have found a source and are confident that it meets the criteria of relevance and credibility from unit 2.2.3. Here is their summary of the source. They have annotated the summary with their analysis.

Why industrial development matters now more than ever before

Manufacturing is the key to economic growth and underpins **inclusive** and sustainable development.

By Li Yong

May 2021

Following a break in popularity in the 1990s, industrial policy is once again capturing attention around the world as a driver of economic and broader societal goals. This is especially true in lower income countries, where industrialisation is still a crucial driver of economic growth.

Moving people out of **informal subsistence farming** into formal manufacturing jobs improves their productivity, makes the agriculture sector more efficient, and raises government revenues through taxation.

There is a strong relationship between poverty reduction and economic growth when that growth is chiefly driven by manufacturing [graph].

So, we need to ramp up support for the industrial sector in developing countries.

Source: The Industrial Analytics Platform, the UNIDO website

This is absolutely relevant to our issue.

This was written to give a pro industry perspective.

Li Yong is Director General of the United Nations Industrial Development Organisation (UNIDO). He has the authority to speak on behalf of an international body. A global issue here so a global perspective.

This is recent enough to take into account the impact of the pandemic.

He is saying that industry is especially important for lower income countries. Will he back this up?

Yes. People who used to farm get jobs in factories and pay taxes. The farmers who stay on the land do a better job. This makes sense – it is a win-win.

There is a graph produced that shows the trend he identifies. The sample was of 40 countries 'for which data on poverty rates for the period 2000–2015 are available'. Date from the UN – but is the sample big enough? How global is it? The evidence provided does back up the claim though.

Conclusion based clearly on the earlier evidence.

Activity: Analysing a written source

2 Work with a partner. Make notes on the following and be ready to share your ideas with another pair or in class discussion.

- **a** Identify who wrote and published this source.
- **b** Explain why Afua and Kwame decided it is a useful source.
- **c** Outline the course of action that is proposed in the source.
- **d** What positive assessments of the source do Afua and Kwame make?
- **e** What aspect(s) of the source are they less confident of?
- **f** What further perspectives would be useful for their research?

Vocabulary

inclusive: If you describe development as inclusive, you mean that it allows all of society to benefit from it, rather than just a minority.

informal subsistence farming: in subsistence farming, farmers produce food to eat themselves rather than to sell, and this work takes place outside of a legal system or a tax system

pro: in favour of

Develop

Here is a graph that Afua and Kwame found in Li Yong's article. It shows the impact of different kinds of economic growth on poverty reduction.

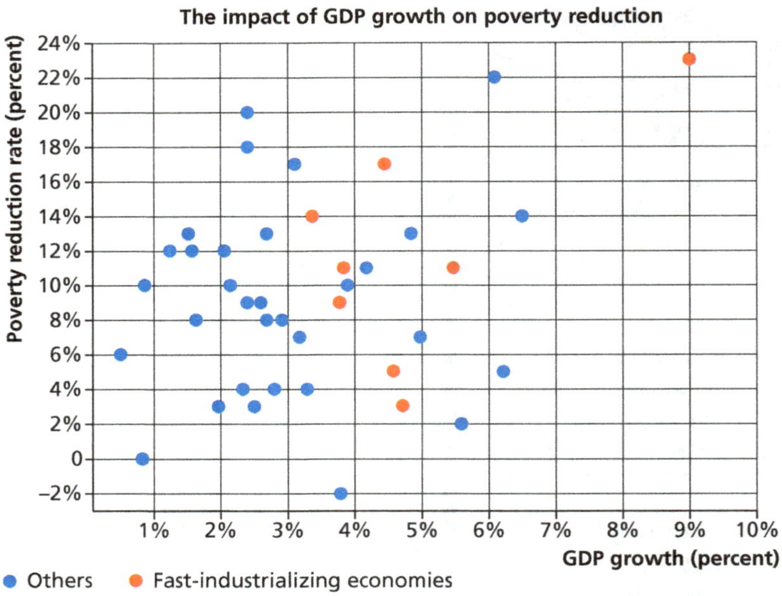

Note: The growth rate is the compound annual growth rate of GDP per capita. The sample consists of 40 countries for which data on poverty raters for the period 2000–2015 are available.
Source: Adaptation based on UNIDO (2020).

Afua and Kwame analysed the graph together. Here is part of their discussion.

Afua:	Hmm… The country with the highest GDP growth is a fast-industrialising economy. That's the one on the top right. It also had the highest poverty reduction.
Kwame:	The country with the lowest GDP growth is not a fast-industrialising economy. That's the one on the bottom left. It also had the lowest poverty reduction. Are we seeing a trend? There is, however, one country that achieved a 22% poverty reduction without industrialising rapidly.
Afua:	I think we have to look at more than single cases. Look. *None* of the countries that grew their economies by *less* than 3% are fast industrialisers. *All* of the fast industrialisers had better growth.
Kwame:	There are only eight out of the 40 countries that industrialised rapidly. Of these eight, five of them had poverty reduction rates of more than 10%. That's good – but not all industrialising countries did so well.
Afua:	What was it Li Yong said? 'There is a *strong* relationship between poverty reduction and economic growth when that growth is *chiefly* driven by manufacturing.' That is borne out, isn't it?
Kwame:	I think so. 'We need to ramp up support for the industrial sector in developing countries' *seems* obvious. What do we think of the sample size though? I'd like to know a bit more about where these countries are and why some did not do so well at poverty reduction.
Afua:	I'm clear about the 'inclusive' growth aspect. I'd like to know more about sustainability.

Activity: Analysing a statistical source

3 Read the conversation above and work with a partner. Make notes and be ready to share your ideas with another pair or in class discussion.

- **a** Identify the information that is provided on the horizontal and vertical axes of the graph.
- **b** Outline the relationship between different factors that is shown in the source.
- **c** Explain why Afua and Kwame would have decided this was useful data for their investigation.
- **d** Summarise the information that is provided by the data in 20 words or less.
- **e** What positive assessments do Afua and Kwame make of how useful this information is to their investigation?
- **f** What aspect(s) of the statistics are they less confident of?
- **g** What further statistical information would be useful for their research?

Apply

Final task

4 You are going to find, discuss and annotate a perspective for an investigation into the question: *Can tourism be sustainable?*

- **a** Search online for 'sustainable tourism'.
- **b** Choose a source that you think offers a relevant and credible perspective (see page 45).
- **c** Summarise the perspective.
- **d** Use these questions to guide a paired discussion:
  - What was positive about the source?
  - What were you less sure of?
  - What further perspectives would be useful for your research?

5 **Challenge:** Try to locate some relevant statistical information.

- **a** Summarise the information that is provided by the data in 20 words or less.
- **b** What positive assessments can you make of how useful this information is to your investigation?
- **c** What aspect(s) of the statistics are you less confident of?
- **d** What further statistical information would be useful for your research?

Reflective plenary

6 Complete these sentences.

You know you have a useful source for your enquiry when…

When you have located a useful source for your enquiry, you should make sure that you…

Setting out courses of action

Skills focus
✓ Analysis, evaluation, communication

Objective
- To learn how to evaluate how courses of action are presented

How can I propose a course of action effectively?

Starting point

1 Think of a situation when a group that you were part of needed to make a decision. How did you decide which option was the best?

Explore

Often when someone holds a perspective on an issue, it leads them to put forward a solution. For instance, in Unit 2.2.2, Manuel Arias advocated the development of a large tourism complex to solve unemployment. In Unit 2.2.4, Li Yong advocated industrialisation as a way of lifting people out of poverty. In this unit, we will focus specifically on finding appropriate courses of action to solve a problem.

Syed and Easton found the following article which was written by the government of the state of Kerala in India. It outlines a strategy to promote tourism while allowing local people to continue with their way of life. The government also wants to ensure that the benefits of tourism are shared.

Vocabulary

Inclusive Growth: If you describe growth as 'inclusive', you mean that it benefits all kinds of people, rather than just one kind of person or a small group of people

phased: staggered or brought about in stages

Kerala's step towards a new tourism culture – 'Street' project

'Street' is the project implemented by the Department of Tourism with an emphasis on traditional lifestyles and rural tourism. [...] The State Responsible Tourism Mission has formulated the Street Project based on the UNWTO's new tourism slogan 'Tourism for **Inclusive Growth**'.

The aim of the project is to set up streets, where the people can see and experience the specifics of each area. Streets such as Green Street, Cultural Street, Ethnic Cuisine / Food Street, Village Life Experience / Experiential Tourism Street, Agri Tourism Street, Water Street, and Art Street will be created as part of the project.

[...]

It is hoped that the project, which will transform each region of Kerala into a tourism street, will lead to major changes and leaps in the tourism sector of Kerala. The project is Kerala's stepping stone to a new tourism culture and it will create large employment opportunities at the local level.

The first phase of the street project is being implemented in locations [including] Kadalundi in Kozhikode district.

[...] The project will be developed in a **phased** manner to help change the face of each area. It is hoped that this will introduce a rural area of Kerala to tourists from all over the world [...], highlighting the uniqueness, taste, and diversity of the country, offering a great income to the local people. It will be a great tourist experience to the tourists who arrive in Kerala.

Source: Official Web Portal. Government of Kerala (India) Published on: 30-11-2021; accessed 31-01-22

Activity: Identifying courses of action

Syed and Easton have begun to highlight the article.

Key:

Green	How the project will be implemented.
Yellow	How the project will address the issues of inclusive growth.

2 What other phrases/sentences could be highlighted green or yellow?

Develop

Activity: Summarising proposed courses of action

3 Work with a partner.

- **a** Summarise the action proposed. Include how the project will be implemented.
- **b** Summarise how the project will address inclusive growth.
- **c** Compare this course of action with the one proposed in source B on page 39 of Unit 2.2.2. List the similarities and differences.

Apply

Final task

Evaluating courses of action

4 Which course of action from activity **3c** do you find more convincing?

Write a paragraph that:

- considers both perspectives
- evaluates their evidence and reasoning
- supports your judgement with their words and ideas.

Reflective plenary

5 Look at this statement: 'Tourism is a much better way to develop a region sustainably and inclusively than the manufacturing industry.'

How has your perspective changed or developed since Unit 2.2.1 as a result of the different perspectives you have explored?

Conducting primary research

Skills focus
✓ Research, analysis

Objective
- To learn how to use primary research methods to investigate perspectives

How can I find out different perspectives for myself?

Starting point

1 If you want to find different local perspectives, it could be useful to do your own primary research. What might the advantages and drawbacks be of working in this way?

Explore

In this unit, you are going to consider what can be learned about different perspectives through first-hand research.

Mansoor and Fiza are classmates. They have been researching the attitudes of students in their final year at school. Mansoor thought that girls would be less likely to consider a job in the manufacturing industry than boys. He also thought that girls would be more likely to consider a job in tourism than boys. Fiza disagreed. They both wanted to find out if boys' and girls' career choices are motivated by different considerations.

They decided to carry out a **survey**. They asked 50 students at lunch break if they would like to take part, and gave **questionnaires** to those who agreed. The questionnaires were colour-coded by gender, but were completed anonymously.

There were five statements on the questionnaires:

1 Working in tourism would give me a good quality of life.
2 The tourism sector offers competitive salaries.
3 Working hours in the tourism industry are fair.
4 Jobs in tourism are secure.
5 I am actively considering a career in tourism.

Each question was followed with these options:

- Strongly Agree ☐
- Agree ☐
- Undecided ☐
- Disagree ☐
- Strongly Disagree ☐

The same five statements were repeated, this time with 'manufacturing' replacing the highlighted word. Each question was followed by the same five options.

The students returned their completed sheets after lunch.

Fourteen boys and eight girls returned their questionnaires. Mansoor and Fiza then used the results to generate statistical information. They presented this information in graphs and used the graphs to draw conclusions.

Key terms

survey: the process of collecting, analysing and interpreting data from a group of people

questionnaire: the term used to describe the set of questions you ask an individual

Activity: Analysing primary research

2 Discuss the following in pairs.

a Mansoor and Fiza tested two predictions. What were they?

b How did Mansoor and Fiza select people to take part in this survey?

c What kind of information does this survey provide?

Develop

Activity: Evaluating research methods

3 Discuss these statements about Mansoor's and Fiza's research methods in your group. Report back to the class whether you agree or disagree, and why.

- **a** Mansoor and Fiza considered their own safety carefully.
- **b** They considered the **ethics** of their research appropriately.
- **c** Repeating the investigation would give the same results.
- **d** The **sample** was **representative** of wider society.
- **e** The survey could be used successfully in another school, in another country.

Here are the responses to two questions in Mansoor's and Fiza's survey.

Working hours in the tourism industry are fair.

Response	Overall	Boys	Girls
Strongly Agree	0	0	0
Agree	5	2	3
Undecided	9	6	3
Disagree	7	5	2
Strongly Disagree	1	1	0
Total	22	14	8

I am actively considering a career in tourism.

Response	Overall	Boys	Girls
Strongly Agree	0	0	0
Agree	4	1	3
Undecided	12	7	5
Disagree	5	5	0
Strongly Disagree	1	1	0
Total	22	14	8

Key terms

ethics: If primary research is conducted ethically, it is done with appropriate consideration for those taking part; ethical considerations include seeking the consent of participants, protecting their personal data and making sure they know that they have a right to withdraw

sample: a number of people chosen from a larger group and used to survey or to provide information about the whole group

representative: accurately represents or reflects

Activity: Drawing conclusions

4 Mansoor says, "Girls are less concerned about working long hours."

- **a** Is it possible to draw this conclusion from this set of results?
- **b** What other explanations are possible?
- **c** What limitations of the research would he need to acknowledge?

Apply

Final task

Conducting a survey

5 Work in small groups.

- **a** Make a prediction about the attitudes *in your class* to working in tourism.
- **b** Devise ten statements to test this prediction.
- **c** Conduct your survey.
- **d** Collect and present your results.
- **e** Present your conclusions.

Reflective plenary

6 Discuss what you have learned so far about the different uses of primary and secondary research methods.

Applying your skills

Skills focus

✓ Research, analysis, evaluation, communication

Objective

- To learn how to communicate a solution to an issue

How can I convince an audience that my course of action would address the issue?

Starting point

1 Who is the most convincing speaker that you have listened to as part of a large audience? What made their speech effective? Discuss in pairs.

Explore

In this section, you will begin by analysing two different arguments about the issue of whether tourism or manufacturing can provide more sustainable and inclusive growth. You will then present your own arguments for a course of action.

Shirin and Abouzar are making presentations to a group of decision-makers from a regional assembly.

Here is part of Shirin's argument that her region should focus on tourism to promote development.

Vocabulary

apprenticeships: a system whereby someone works for a fixed period of time in a job or industry in order to be trained and learn the skills needed

> It has become more common for less economically developed countries and regions to focus successful development policies on tourism. Put simply, it changes lives. Local people develop a better understanding of diverse visitors. Studies conducted by the University of Pintado in the 1960s, when the sector started taking off, found that people working in the sector frequently learned new language skills, and this built their self-esteem.
>
> Promoting tourism will raise our people's expectations. As people from around the world connect with natural wonders here, people from the region will take pride in their local environment. This strategy will accelerate socio-economic growth, job creation and income generation.

Here is part of Abouzar's argument that his region should focus on industry to promote development.

> It is a matter of grave concern that we are considering turning our backs on the manufacturing sector that has been vital for this region. Do we not need to remember that the impact of air travel on CO_2 emissions is increasing every year?
>
> Work in tourism is seasonal. Work in industry is stable. 5000+ opportunities for young people were provided right across our region through industrial **apprenticeships** last year. Can tourism match that commitment to skills?
>
> We can choose the path of sustainable industrial development. Funding is available to build clean, low-carbon production facilities. The success of over 150 projects in over 60 countries proves that this approach works.

Activity: Evaluating arguments

2 What claims does Shirin make? What evidence and reasoning does she offer in support? What about Abouzar? Whose argument do you find more convincing? Explain your answer.

Develop

Imagine you live in a rural area that has been awarded development money to grow its economy. You will be supporting one of two proposals.

Proposal A: The money should be spent on tourism development. An eco-tourism resort should be built using local materials and techniques. Local people will get jobs teaching tourists new skills in farming and fishing. Tourists that visit the resort will be required to use sustainable transport.

Proposal B: The money should be invested in a solar energy complex. An engineering park will be attached to the complex to make use of the abundant clean energy. Local people will gain new jobs manufacturing components for electric vehicles. Companies that set up at the park will be required to train local workers.

Activity: Planning a presentation

3 Your group's task is to persuade the regional assembly that your proposal would be more effective at promoting sustainable and inclusive growth. Use the grid to help you plan and draw on the research, analysis and evaluation of sources you have done throughout the investigation.

	Claim	Evidence	Reasoning
A. Eco-tourism			
B. Solar-powered engineering			

Apply

Final task

4 Rehearse, then deliver your presentation. Every member of the group should be involved.

Reflective plenary

5 What was effective about your presentation? What would you do differently next time?

6 Which of the other groups' presentations was most effective? Why?

Check your progress

By the end of this chapter, you should have learned how to:

- develop research questions
- identify perspectives in sources
- analyse and evaluate sources
- develop a line of reasoning to support a course of action
- conduct some primary research on an issue
- communicate a course of action to an audience.

Next steps

- Research the issue of sustainable development further and challenge yourself to find a wider range of local, national and global perspectives on this issue. What is the best way to promote economic development and protect the environment at the same time? How can we make sure that the benefits of economic development are shared fairly?

- Look out for other discussions of global issues; you can find different perspectives in podcasts, radio and television broadcasts, or a range of online platforms. Very often, if someone is putting forward a perspective on an issue, they will offer solutions too. As you encounter different perspectives, ask yourself how persuaded you are by them. Is the evidence clear? Are they based on sound logic? To what extent does the perspective on the issue reflect what you know to be true? Keep reflecting on how your own perspective changes or develops in response to these different arguments.

Section 2: Developing key skills

Investigation 3: How can our team provide support for a local vulnerable group?

2.3

This investigation will explore the issue of caring for the vulnerable in society, using your research skills. You will be asked to decide your viewpoint and to come to a conclusion. As part of your investigation, you will work with a team, collaborate to make a difference to a local issue, and design a means of showing others what you have achieved.

The investigation will focus on the syllabus topics: 'Social identity and inclusion'. It will also touch on 'Health and wellbeing'; 'Political power and action'; 'Poverty and inequality'; and 'Values and beliefs'.

Your final task will be to evaluate what you achieved as a team and your own role in the project.

This investigation focuses on collaboration, communication, analysis, evaluation and reflection. You will be developing the following skills:

3.1 Identifying an issue, points of view and teamwork

3.2 Researching an issue as a team

3.3 Deciding on and taking an action

3.4 Providing evidence of an action

3.5 Reflecting on teamwork

3.6 Applying what you have learned.

Identifying an issue, points of view and teamwork

Skills focus
✓ Collaboration, reflection, communication

Objective
- To collaborate to identify a shared topic of interest
- To plan and communicate as part of a team

How can I work in a team to agree a local issue to research?

Starting point

1 In pairs, discuss the viewpoints below.
   a Which viewpoints are about issues that interest you most? Can you think of other issues to do with vulnerable groups in your local area?
   b Organise yourselves into teams of between two and five members. Work with others who share an interest in similar issues from activity **1a**.

Caring for elderly people in society

We have had a good reputation of family care for our parents. This is changing. Families can no longer afford to pay for this care. Our government must do something to help us.

Caring for homeless people

33% of homeless people are there because of domestic violence and relationship breakdown. It is not their fault. They need help.

Caring for refugees

In my head, I am still a little boy seeing so much damage to my town. We fled to Syria and my family set up a hairdressing business. Then it all went wrong again. I am happy with my family in Turkey, where I am being supported to train to be a teacher.

Explore

A team of students is planning a project. Read the extracts below taken from two of their meetings.

Meeting 1

Sara: We should look at helping people our own age as we would understand them.

Sitara: My sister said that we should work with a group that is safe for us. We should not do anything dangerous. But I do feel sorry for people who are refugees from their own countries.

Nadia: We have to discuss the idea with our teacher. He won't let us do anything stupid.

Sara: Shall we go away and look at which children locally need help of some sort?

Asal: Would anyone object if I reach out to a school near here where refugee children are staying? Just to find out what the situation is.

Iroda: That sounds like a plan. Before we go, should we make sure we know who is making notes of what we do? I will do that, if you want me to.

Nadia: That's a good idea. Who do you think should be team leader? Someone who can keep us on track? I'd be no good at that.

Sitara: Sara has kept us in order so far. Would you chair our meetings?

Meeting 2

Nadia: My dad said that lots of refugees find fitting into education difficult. I have talked to the school psychologist to see what she knows. She says the big problem for young people who are refugees in our schools is that they don't feel they fit in because they don't know our culture or much about our country. The schools they are in are great, but we could help.

Iroda: We can't do anything that would help with such a big problem, surely?

Sitara: I don't know about that. Doesn't our notice board show how the UN is giving laptops to help refugees with education? I talked to our school nurse. She says we could ask to use the school messaging system, if we wanted to.

Asal: Well, we can't buy computers, that's for sure. But that school I was talking about? They would welcome some help. They agree with what you found out, Nadia. It is just about making friends with others and making young people feel welcome.

Sara: What could we do?

The team then discussed these ideas:

- raise money by selling cakes or books
- have a sports day in school, inviting refugee families
- have a day in school to talk with the children who are refugees and make them welcome
- write to teenaged children who are refugees. Be a pen pal, possibly using email or messaging.

They talked to their teacher who said he thought it would be impossible to bring young people into school for one day because they are so spread out across the country. But he thought organising pen pals was a great idea.

Iroda:	How does having a pen pal help a young person who is a refugee? It doesn't seem to be doing much!
Sitara:	How would you like to be away from your friends? At least you wouldn't feel so isolated if you knew some young people in your new country, even if only by letter.
Sara:	OK, that seems to work. Do we all agree? Let's research how we could find out about contacting refugee teenagers and whether there is anything to say that refugees want pen pals.
Iroda:	If the UN has a perspective on this; if our town has a perspective on this…
Sitara:	… what parents think about us contacting young people and is our school happy for us to invite others to be pen pals?
Iroda:	Let me write those ideas down. We should all take one thing to find out before we meet again.

Activity: Investigating how to plan a project

2 a What are the team discussing in each meeting?

b Did this team collaborate and communicate effectively? Complete this grid.

	Yes/No	Comment
Did they do some initial research?		
Did they make a decision to identify a clear **aim** for the project? Was it reached through discussion?		
Did they **take turns** in discussion? Is everyone involved in both meetings, using **active listening**?		
Did individuals in the group listen to each other actively, share ideas and respond to other people's suggestions?		
Are they organised as a team? Do they have team roles (e.g. **chair**, **scribe**, **specialist**)? Do they take notes or **minutes**? Do they agree what to do, who will do it and when?		
Have they **collaborated** by completing their research tasks?		
Have they made sure their project is acceptable? Have they checked with the teacher?		

Key terms

aim: what you are hoping to achieve through a project

take turns: when people in a team listen to one person at a time; when another person has their turn, the team listens to that speaker; everyone is expected to speak and to be listened to

active listening: as people are speaking, the team takes their ideas and discusses them further to move the meeting forward

chair: calls meetings and makes sure that the aims of the meeting are met

scribe: notes key points, ideas and decisions, adding who made them

specialist: person with skills that will be useful, e.g. IT skills, artistic skills, ability to speak confidently in public, ability to ask questions

take minutes: noting the key points that are said in a meeting, especially any decisions made or ideas that are put forward

collaborated: when two or more individuals work together to solve a problem; collaboration is similar to cooperation; most collaboration requires some form of leadership

Develop

Reflection on how your team works and your own role in it will help you to understand and improve the team's effectiveness, and make sure you get the best out of everyone. You are going to do this by writing a log of reflections as you work through the project.

Key terms

reflection: thinking about or considering something in depth

Activity: Starting to keep a reflective log

This reflection from Iroda focuses only on the good things about her contribution.

I think I did quite well in the first two meetings we had. I offered to keep notes of our decisions and who contributed to them. This suited me as I would worry if I left this to someone else. I am pleased no one expected me to be leader. But I think I helped to clarify our aim, and why it will make a difference to some young people who are refugees.

3 With your team, discuss any points Iroda should consider in order to improve her contribution to the next team meeting.

Reflections should recognise strengths and weaknesses. No contribution is perfect, nor worthless.

Apply

Final task

Understanding more about your vulnerable group

4 You're ready now to make a start on a team project. Work in your team of between two and five people who share an interest in helping a vulnerable group in your local community. Hold your first meeting:

- Discuss how you will organise your group, what roles you will have, and how you will keep team notes of discussions and decisions.
- Decide on a vulnerable group you might want to help. Work out who has a perspective on the issues facing this group, and what you want to find out. At this early stage, think about local people in your community who might have expertise: school psychologist, parents, grandparents, head teacher or someone else in your local community.
- Plan to hold a second meeting to share your initial research findings.

Reflective plenary

5 Log your reflections of the part you took in these discussions to show your contributions, your ideas, how you supported others and how others supported you. Use the grid from activity **2b** to guide you.

Researching an issue as a team

Skills focus
✓ Collaboration, communication, research, reflection

Objective
- To communicate and collaborate to plan your research tasks
- To reflect on your teamwork and progress, and log your thoughts

How can I work in a team to plan our project research?

Starting point

1 a In your team, remind yourselves of what you agreed to be the focus of your project so far. Confirm that it suits everyone.

b Put your aim into words. It could be something like: *Find out more about the needs of young refugees and decide on which course of action meets these needs.*

c What ideas do you have about how to support the group you have chosen?
- Do you want to inform people of something?
- Do you want to improve a situation?
- Do you want to give opportunities for some people to do something?
- Or... something else?

Explore

The case study team from Unit 2.3.1 agreed that their aim was to help support students who were refugees and feeling isolated in their community.

They had begun to look at how they might do this and wanted to find out whether a pen pals project might be appropriate and manageable. The next stage was to carry out further research into the needs of refugee students and into pen pals.

The team came up with a list of questions to research, as follows:

- *How could we find out about contacting teenagers who are refugees? Maybe start with the school nearby.*
- *Is there anything to say refugees want pen pals?*
- *Does the UN have a perspective on this?*
- *Do we need anybody's approval? Like the approval of the* ***NGO*** *working with these young people?*
- *Does our town have a perspective on this?*
- *What do our parents think about us contacting these young people?*
- *Is our school happy for us to invite others to be pen pals?*

Vocabulary

NGO: a non-profit organisation that furthers some social or humanitarian missions around the globe

Activity: Identifying what group research needs to be done

2 a Iroda suggested that they should each take one of the questions (on page 62) to research. Does your team agree? Is there one particular question that everyone should ask?

b Why is it important to have the head teacher's approval before you write to anyone outside your school?

c Are there any questions you would add or remove from the other group's list?

d Asking a search engine for 'NGOs about pen pals for refugee children' yielded several websites. Can you find one?

e Asking a search engine 'Do refugees want a pen pal?' located many websites. Can you find one?

f Try asking a search engine: 'Does the UN have a view about pen pals for refugees?' to see if you can find a UN perspective.

Develop

If you are involved in a team project with a social purpose, you will need to make sure that you do it safely and that you consider the ethics of your research. When you are considering what to research and any courses of action you might take, you should always check with your teacher first.

Activity: Conducting research safely and ethically

3 a What might the students in the case study do to keep themselves and their pen pals safe? What will you do in your team to keep yourselves, and the people you want to help, safe?

b Read the advice below and discuss in your group how you can make sure your research project is ethical.

Some ethical considerations:

Participation should be *voluntary* and people you ask should know why you are asking. This means that letters or emails should make clear what you are planning. You should be able to use your school's name in your letters – with permission from your head teacher.

Participants should have *anonymity* and *confidentiality*. If you want to be able to use their names in your project reports, then you must ask for their permission.

Some research carries a *potential for harm*. It is not likely from your research, but people have been known to give answers that could make their lives difficult. You should not put people at risk.

You must always *communicate results*. You need to share research findings. Note: Honesty matters. If your parents do not approve of what your team wants to do, you must make sure that your team knows that you cannot be involved.

Apply

Final task

Initial research, feedback and planning further research

4 You have already decided on a local issue that you are interested in, and you will have conducted some initial research by asking people in the community what they know about your chosen vulnerable group and their needs.

a Hold a meeting in which each member of the team feeds back what they have found out.

Make a note of the different perspectives.

b Agree in your team what the issues facing this vulnerable group might be. Make a list or a spider diagram.

c Further research:

- Agree together which of these issues would be good to investigate further, and write a list of questions to research.
- Think about any possible actions you might take to help support your vulnerable group – to raise money or raise awareness through a social media campaign, for example.
- How are you going to find out if there is a global perspective on the issue? Remember to make your question as refined as you can when asking a search engine.
- How do you find out if what you are interested in really is needed?
- How do you make a start on seeing if your project is possible? Is there someone local that you need to speak to?

d Share this work between the team, then agree a deadline and a date for the next meeting.

Checklist for success

✔ Remember to appoint a chair for your meeting and someone to scribe.

✔ Listen actively and make sure everyone gets to contribute.

Reflective plenary

5 Keep a note in your reflective log of the part you played in these discussions to show your contributions, your ideas, how you supported others and how others supported you.

Comment on the research and whether you think proposed solutions will be helpful.

Record details of what you did well in this meeting and what you could do better next time.

Deciding on and taking an action

How can I use our research to identify and carry out an appropriate course of action?

Once the members of your team have completed their research tasks, you will be ready to agree on what **action** you would like to take. This means doing a practical thing to make a difference to the problems or issue you have identified.

Starting point

1 In your group, brainstorm activities that you are able to carry out to make a difference to the problem you have identified.

You will already have come up with some possible actions that might help you to support your vulnerable group. Would any of these actions be relevant to your aims? Can you add any additional ones?

- holding a sale to raise money
- organising an online chat or befriending events
- setting up a social media campaign
- posting leaflets
- organising a visiting rota
- writing to an MP
- inviting speakers to the school
- holding an information event

Skills focus

✓ Collaboration, research, analysis, communication

Objective

- To communicate to share findings from research
- To collaborate to identify an appropriate action to help with the issue
- To plan and organise the action

Key terms

action: in Global Perspectives, an action is something the team does to improve or find a solution to a local issue; for example, an action to respond to the issue of loneliness in elderly people in the community might be to set up a rota of visits.

Explore

Activity: Listening to findings from individual research

2 Read the research findings below from the case study team (Unit 2.3.1). Discuss in pairs whether you think that the pen pals project will be practical and will meet the aims of the team.

At **Meeting 3**, the case study team reported back and shared their research findings:

- *Asking a search engine for 'NGOs about pen pals for refugee children'*

  Sara had found a website they could go to in order to find out who is in charge of this in their country. She shared the website address. She had made contact and they would be able to do that, if they still wanted to.
- *Asking a search engine 'Do refugees want a pen pal?'*

  Asal had not found reports from their country but had found reports from many other countries that suggested they would be appreciated.
- *Asking a search engine: 'Does the UN have a view about pen pals for refugees?'*

  Nadia was not able to find a UN statement, but, as most of the websites she found were linked to the UN, she could only assume they would be in favour.
- *Asking a search engine: 'How do we contact refugees if we want to become penpals?'*

  Sitara found that it was not difficult to become a pen pal. Worried about having to find the teenagers themselves, she had contacted an NGO through a search engine, and been given assurance that the NGO would make first contact with the teenagers' school. The head teacher was pleased with their initiative and gave permission for the team to go forward.

Develop

At Meeting 3, Sara asked the team to look at tasks that needed to be done, to find who was suited to each task.

They came up with the following ideas.

- Use noticeboards around school to put up information and find students to write the letters.
- Use the school website to share what they were planning and to ask for volunteers.
- Contact the NGO to confirm that letters would be written and to ask for names of teenagers.

This meant they needed team members to:

- Make posters. **Asal** offered to use design software to make them because she knew how.
- Put up the finished posters. **Iroda** offered to do this.
- Post onto the school website. **Asal** offered to do this.
- Contact the NGO. **Sitara** said she would do this as she had already found the contact details.
- Get approval from the head teacher. **Asal** offered to do this.
- Keep a list of volunteers. **Iroda** offered as she was keeping minutes of meetings, and so had all the documents.
- Write a letter to encourage others to join in. **Sara** said she would write one, and asked **Nadia** to write a different one. That way they would have two to share. And everyone would have a job.

Iroda suggested using a spreadsheet to keep track of their tasks and progress.

	A	B	C	D	E	F
1						
2		**Action**	**Who**	**Date to be completed**	**Approved by school**	**Ticked off as done**
3		Make posters	Asal			
4		Put posters up around school	Iroda			
5		Make a post for the school website	Asal			
6		Contact the local NGO for approval	Sitara			
7		Write letters to show to volunteers	Sara Nadia			
8		Get school approval	Asal			
9		Keep a list of volunteers and make notes available to the team	Iroda			

Activity: Planning and allocating tasks (case study)

3 Discuss what you think of the case study team's plans and how they have organised themselves.

Apply

You should now be at a stage where you can confirm your research findings and begin to plan your activity for your team project.

Activity: Reviewing your own research

4 Start by reviewing the plans you made in Meeting 2. Who was answering each research question?

- **a** Share your findings. Start by stating the question. Then, give your first research finding in your own words.
- **b** After listening, team members can ask questions, one at a time. Go slowly. Make sure your scribe can take notes!
- **c** Repeat, going through each research question.
- **d** Finally, review: Has your research shown that your idea was a useful one? If the answer is 'yes', then carry on. If it is 'no', then start again. This is a good time to talk to your teacher, to make sure your plans will keep you safe.

Final task

5 Make detailed plans about actions and who is to carry them out, by holding a meeting.

- Discuss and agree on a course of action that will support the needs of this group and your project aim.
- Plan what you need to do to achieve your action. What tasks need doing? Who will do what? What equipment do you need? When will you need to complete each task? When will you next need to meet? How will you communicate?
- Record this information on a grid or spreadsheet.

Reflective plenary

6 Keep a note in your reflective log of the part you took in this work to show your contributions, your ideas, how you supported others and how others supported you.

Record details of what you did well in this meeting and what you could do better next time.

Do you think the action will meet your team aims?

Providing evidence of an action

Skills focus

✓ Collaboration, communication

Objective

- To understand how to collaborate to identify an appropriate way of showing others the issue and your action/achievement
- To improve your ability to communicate to share ideas

How can our team show evidence of what we have done?

As a part of your project, you will need to document what you have done, and provide evidence of what your team's action was. This isn't evidence of research or initial meetings, and it isn't intended as evaluation; it is simply to provide evidence of what action you have taken. The type of evidence you provide will depend on the project and the action you take, though it is often a good idea to take photographs, if you can.

Starting point

1 In your team, make a quick list of the types of evidence that might suit your project.

For example:

photographs

a poster.

Explore

Activity: Investigating how to evidence actions

2 Before you take your team action, you should consider how you are going to provide evidence of it. Look at the case study below. What is good about their plans and what could be improved?

Case study team: Meeting 4

Sara: We don't seem to have a lot to show for our project. How can we show people about it? I can only think that we have our letters.

Nadia: I think the letters are just what we need, though. This isn't about research, it's just to show what our action was – so evidence that we set up a pen pal project. Maybe we could also show copies of our data – how many students volunteered and how many links we've made to teenagers who are refugees. Perhaps we could display the letters and data on a PowerPoint slide?

Iroda: Yes, that sounds good.

Sitara: If we have any replies by then, we could add parts of a reply that someone received from a pen pal. Would that be on another slide?

Asal: Definitely. That's more important than our letters.

Dear student,

My name is Asal, and I would like to be your pen pal.

My school is big as well. We stay here during the term and most of us go home for holidays. I guess you stay in school, too? The food is awful in school – nothing like Mum's cooking. Is your food what you are used to?

We get some free time and listen to bands. What is your favourite music? I like songs I can sing along to.

To: Asal

Subject: Continue writing

Hi Asal,

Thank you for writing to me. My friends have had letters from your school as well. We would like to carry on writing to you. It is useful emailing as we can improve our language.

We stay in school. Most children here go home, but there are some, like us, who live here. I don't know yet if they go home for the holidays.

The food is nothing like I am used to. There is so much fish here. But it is tasty and we enjoy it. Does everyone eat so much?

Develop

Activity: Final planning and action

3 a In your team, agree how you will evidence your action, and identify who will do what.

Plan whether you are going to show your class, your school or someone else, what you have done.

b Complete your final planning for your action, adding in details of any evidence that will need to be collected.

Apply

Final task

4 a Carry out the activity or action that your team has planned.

b Collect and display your evidence as a team so that everyone is satisfied.

Reflective plenary

5 Keep note of the part you took in your team's action to show your contributions, your ideas, your actions, how you supported others and how others supported you.

Record details of what you did well in the final planning meeting and what you think could have been better.

Reflecting on teamwork

Skills focus
✓ Evaluation, reflection

Objective
- To evaluate your team's course of action
- To evaluate how effectively you worked with your team

How can I evaluate the success of my project?

Now that you have completed your action, you are going to be asked to evaluate how effective your project was in relation to its aims, and how effectively you worked with your team.

Starting point

1 With a partner, consider what you understand by the term **evaluation**. What were your team's aims for this project? (You may need to remind yourself of this by looking at the Starting point in Unit 2.3.2.)

Key terms

evaluation: an appraisal of something to determine its worth/effectiveness for purpose

Explore

Read what these students from the case study team said about their action. Their stated aim was to: *Find out more about the needs of young people who are refugees and decide on which course of action meets these needs.*

Iroda: We did what we said we would do. Our letters had replies and the teenagers were pleased to have someone to write to. They said we were like new friends.

Asal: Our project was successful. We sent ten letters to different teenagers and had nine replies. The nine replies hoped that we would write again.

Sara: We met our aims of supporting teenaged refugees by becoming their pen pals. The nine letters we have had back (in response to ten sent) said they wanted to be friends and hoped we would write again. This shows they valued our contact. It was sad that we only got five more students to write letters to them. This shows that our methods of getting people interested were not very good. We would have to work harder at this if we did it again.

it is very clear how far the project was successful

evidence to show the project went well

a limitation of the project – didn't fully achieve the team's aims

the team are learning about what should be done differently in future projects

Activity: Evaluating an action (case study)

2 a Which one of these three students has evaluated their project? Explain why.

b What have the other two missed out?

c Look at Sara's answer. What would have been a better suggested improvement than: 'We would have to work harder at this if we did it again'?

Develop

Now read what these students said about how they contributed to the case study team.

Sitara:	I was good at listening and taking my turn. It made meetings effective, so decisions were made. I mostly did what I said I would do. I noticed that no one had agreed to get the school's approval for the project, so I did that on top of my own work. I should have made sure that Iroda knew that I was doing this, but I forgot. What we didn't do very well was review each other's work. I should have noticed that no one had put a poster up in my classroom. Then I could have let Iroda or Sara know. We didn't get enough volunteers early on, and we should have realised. This meant we only had ten letters – not enough to make things better on a wider scale!
Sara:	Overall, our team worked well together. We shared the work and were grateful that others did their parts. None of us could have done all the research or carried out all the tasks on our own.

a strength with evidence

specific example of what they did well

personal failing explained

this would come under failing to support each other and is well evidenced

this is an impact of not doing well; it also refers to their aim of making a difference to teenage refugees' lives

Activity: Evaluating your part in a team (case study)

3 a In what ways is Sitara's evaluation of her role in teamwork better than Sara's?

b Has Sitara mentioned all of the characteristics that make an effective team? For example: listening, taking turns to speak, supporting team members, valuing others' contributions, meeting obligations on time, working as a team member.

Apply

Now that you have considered the case study team's evaluation of the effectiveness of their action in relation to their aims and how effective the individuals' own contributions were, you are going to begin to evaluate your own action and contribution to your team project.

Final task

Evaluating our team's course of action and my part in the team

4 How effectively did your action meet the aims that you set yourself? Think about your aims.

- **a** What were the team's aims?
- **b** To what extent did the team's course of action meet the aims agreed by the team?
- **c** What went well? What is your evidence for saying so?
- **d** What could have been better? What is your evidence for saying so?
- **e** Now read back through the thoughts that you logged in the Reflective plenaries for each unit and add any relevant information or evidence from your log to your notes.

5 How effectively did you contribute to the team, and how well did you manage your own tasks?

- **a** Summarise the information or data you gathered in your part of the team's research. Did the team use this information? How?
- **b** Think about your role in the team.
  - Did you carry out the tasks assigned to you effectively, and on time?
  - Did your research contribute to the team's understanding?
  - How did you help the team achieve its aims?
  - Did you support the other team members?
- **c** Read back through the thoughts that you logged in the Reflective plenaries for each unit, to gather relevant information to evaluate your own contribution to the team and its aims. Then add any other notes.
- **d** Make a note of evidence that you can use in writing your evaluation. You will need to provide evidence for both your strengths and weaknesses.

Reflective plenary

6 Share your notes with a partner and discuss their feedback.

Applying what you have learned

Skills focus

✓ Communicating information and reasoning; reflecting on processes and on own learning; researching, analysing and evaluating information

Objective

- To learn how to write up your reflections in a well-structured, supported piece of writing

How can I write a clearly structured reflection?

In this unit, you are going to draw together your evaluation of the success of the project and your role in it, along with other learning and reflections from the project. You are then going to structure them into a piece of reflective writing.

Starting point

1 With a partner, spend a couple of minutes reflecting on the project you've just completed. What did you enjoy? What have you learned about the topic and your chosen issue?

Explore

You will be using the headings below to structure your written reflections. Here, the students from the case study team are gathering their thoughts and writing notes under each heading.

1) Introduction

Outline briefly the aims of your research, and what course of action your team took to achieve the aims.

> Sitara: My team started by researching the vulnerable groups in our country. This showed us that there were teenage refugees in a nearby city. We wanted to help these young people to be happy in our country. Our action was to become pen pals with them, giving them virtual friends outside of their school.

2) Summary of your research

This could be a table, data or a summary of what you found out and from where.

> *Nadia: I started by interviewing my dad. He said that all refugees must feel isolated in a new country. I then interviewed our school nurse and she told me of the difficulty some new arrivals have with small things, such as how we live, what we wear. Everything is strange: their school, the food, the music people listen to.*

3) Reflection on your personal learning

Start by giving a summary of the whole experience: Did you enjoy it? Did you struggle? Did you feel valued?

Then look at what you learned about:

- the issue

> Asal: Refugees who have found a home in a new country are safe, but they are vulnerable because everything is strange to them, and they can feel isolated. I was surprised to find out how many NGOs are involved with refugees. Online communication is really valuable.

- teamwork

> *Iroda: I have learned that support for a team is not just in meetings. We should have kept an eye on the project and made sure there were no gaps in our actions.*

- yourself

> Nadia: *I thought I worked best on my own but I have found that I enjoy working in a team. It isn't always easier to be in a team. Yes, you share the research and don't have to do all the jobs. But it is more demanding in keeping the momentum going when everyone has other work to do.*

4) Evaluation

You completed this evaluation work in the previous unit on page 74. You will need to evaluate:

- the course of action you took and how it met your aims
- how effectively you worked as part of the team and completed your tasks.

Develop

Activity: Gathering evidence

2 Read back through the thoughts that you logged in the Reflective plenaries for each unit to gather relevant information to evaluate your own contribution to the team and its aims. Then add any other notes.

What have I learned...	Notes to include
about the issue and perspectives on it	
about effective teamwork	
about my own skills	
from the whole experience	

Apply

Final task

3 Once you have gathered all your thoughts and have notes under each heading, write up your reflections in paragraphs. Keep the headings in place.

Reflective plenary

4 Exchange your work with a partner. Is your learning similar or have you taken a different learning from the project?

Check your progress

By the end of this chapter, you should have learned how to:

- identify an issue and different perspectives on it
- research the issue to decide on a local project, as part of a team
- decide on and take action to improve the issue
- provide evidence of the action that you have taken
- reflect on teamwork, your personal contribution and how your understanding of the issue has developed.

Next steps

- The skills you have learned are skills that you will use in all your schoolwork and in your social life. Observe yourself as you work with others. Are you actively listening? Are you engaging with their thoughts or too busy planning yours? Do you meet your commitments? Do you communicate effectively with others, in a timely manner?

- What else has caught your interest in this chapter? Were you inspired to explore the world of volunteering or international aid, or perhaps to find out about careers within it? Or is blogging or writing a personal article arguing a point of view on this issue a skill you'd like to develop?

- Make a note of one or two ideas about working in a team or with others that you'd like to share and how you might do so.

Section 2: Developing key skills

2.4 Investigation 4: Should the global fashion industry change the way it operates?

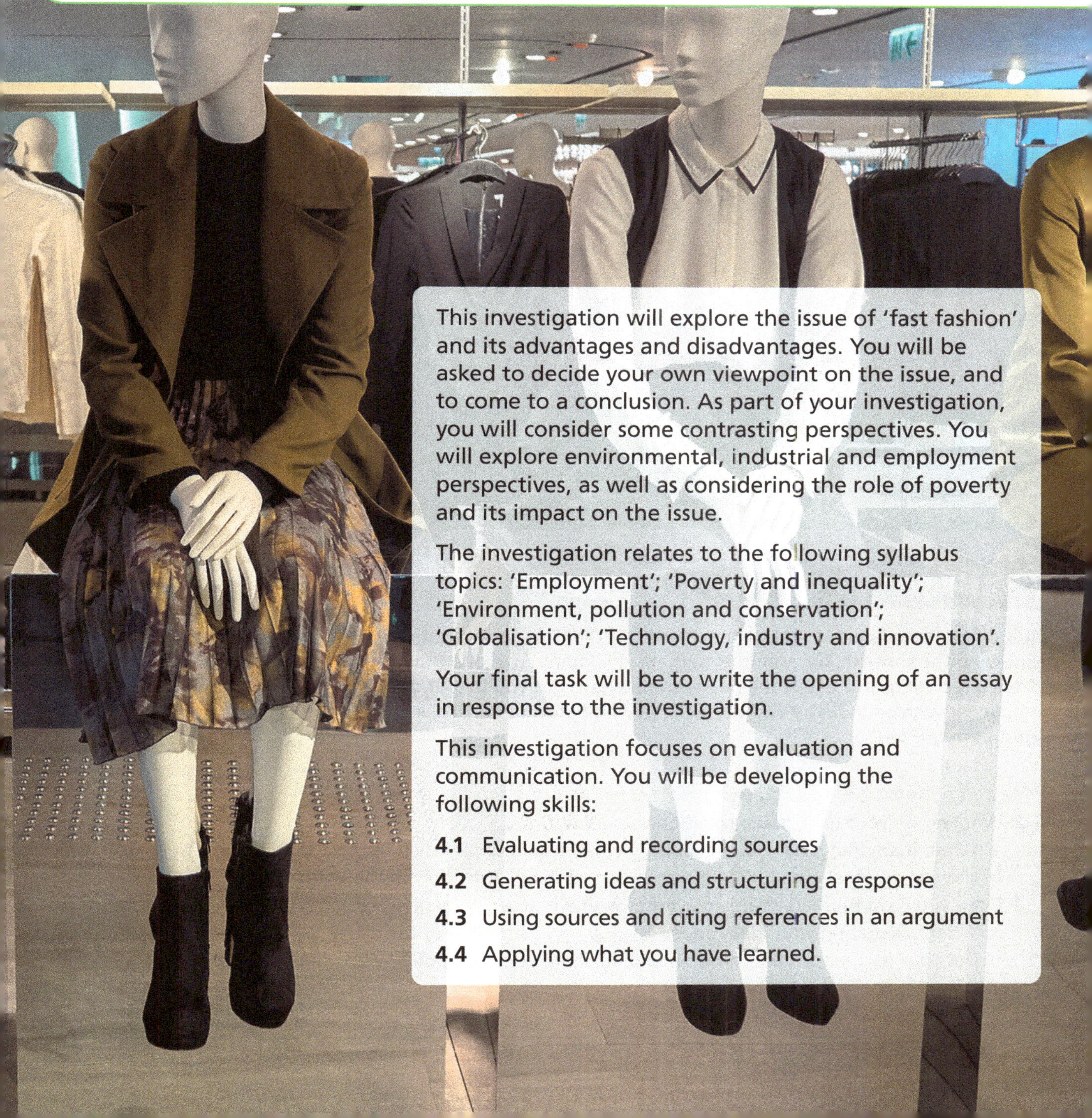

This investigation will explore the issue of 'fast fashion' and its advantages and disadvantages. You will be asked to decide your own viewpoint on the issue, and to come to a conclusion. As part of your investigation, you will consider some contrasting perspectives. You will explore environmental, industrial and employment perspectives, as well as considering the role of poverty and its impact on the issue.

The investigation relates to the following syllabus topics: 'Employment'; 'Poverty and inequality'; 'Environment, pollution and conservation'; 'Globalisation'; 'Technology, industry and innovation'.

Your final task will be to write the opening of an essay in response to the investigation.

This investigation focuses on evaluation and communication. You will be developing the following skills:

4.1 Evaluating and recording sources

4.2 Generating ideas and structuring a response

4.3 Using sources and citing references in an argument

4.4 Applying what you have learned.

Evaluating and recording sources

Skills focus
✓ Evaluation, communication, reflection

Objective
- To refresh your skills of analysis and evaluation
- To apply effective note-taking and logging strategies

How do I record and track my evaluation of sources?

In this unit, you will explore your own perspective, and those of others, on the fashion industry. In particular, you will consider the widespread practice of mass-producing items at low cost in response to rapidly changing trends.

Starting point

1 Look at this image.

a Who might have thrown clothes away like this? Why?
b What do you do with clothes you no longer need?
c Is there any other way this image could be interpreted? (Have they really been 'thrown away'?)

Explore

It is difficult to draw too many conclusions from the image without knowing the context. For example, perhaps the 'dump' was overflow from a recycling centre. But the image should have got you thinking about the fashion industry and what the buying habits of particular groups might be.

Vocabulary

fast fashion: the practice of mass-producing clothes quickly and cheaply

Activity: Sharing ideas and perspectives

2 Working on your own, make notes on these questions.
  a What, if anything, do you know about what is sometimes called the **fast fashion** industry?
  b How do you feel about it? Is it a good or bad thing? Why do you think this?

3 Once you have finished, share your notes with a partner or small group.
  a What has sharing your ideas added to your understanding of the issue?
  b Did your partner or other group members share your viewpoint? What did they base it on?

If your view is based on evidence and reasoning, you could say that it is more than just a viewpoint: it is a perspective.

When you discuss ideas in this way, it is helpful to keep a record. This record will be very useful if and when you need to speak about, write or present your ideas to others.

You can make notes in lots of ways but using a table or a **log** can be helpful. Here is one example of a log, made by a student called Carla, based on the tasks you have just completed.

Key terms

log: a written record of ideas or information

helps track the order of research | reminder of what the focus was | source could be a photo, article, survey or piece of data | general record of what you found out or points raised | next steps

Date/time and place	Task	Source (where relevant)	My notes	Action?
04/06/22 Lesson 2 School	Personal response to 'fast fashion'	Photo of dumped clothes	• Clothes easily thrown away • 'Fast fashion' = producing clothes quickly, cheaply • Good if it makes nice clothes available at a low cost	Task – find out more about 'fast fashion' and why some people feel the need to change or get rid of clothes so quickly
04/06/22 Lesson 2 School	Group chat – what do others think?	Same source	• Delima said massive factory in our town – lots of employment • Jyoti said this was good – but wages quite low	

Activity: Focus on communication

4 Complete a log like the one above to record your own group's thoughts based on activity 3. What might be the next steps you need to take to find out more about this issue?

Language support

When you make notes for a 'thinking' task like this, there are various methods you can use. You can use a mind map to generate a range of initial ideas. Or, if you wish to be more selective or prioritise particular thoughts, you can use bullet points or numbers.

Develop

You may already have your own perspective on the fashion industry but, as the student's log showed, your next action is to find out more. This means asking yourself the following questions.

- Do I fully understand the issues around how the fashion industry operates? Was my understanding – and our group's understanding – accurate?
- If I am trying to understand whether it is a 'good' or 'bad' thing, who might have information or a perspective about this?

In trying to answer these questions, you come across the following page from a website.

Through the Alliance, the UN commits to changing the path of fashion, reducing its negative environmental and social impacts; and turning fashion into a driver of the implementation of the Sustainable Development Goals.

The Clothing and Textile Industry Today...

Contributes $2.4 trillion to global manufacturing

Employs 300 million people worldwide across the value chain (many of them women)

Is responsible for an estimated 2-8% of the world's greenhouse gas emissions

Around 215 trillion liters of water per year are consumed by the industry

Annual material loss of US $100 billion due to underutilisation

Textiles account for approximately 9% of annual microplastic losses to the oceans

Source: from the website of the United Nations Alliance for Sustainable Fashion

Activity: Focus on analysis and evaluation

5 Read the source carefully, and then work with a partner to answer these questions.

a Is it going to help me answer the question I am investigating? (What information does it reveal? Does it tell me anything about the fashion industry?)

b Who – or what organisation – has produced this source? Can I trust it? What is the writer's expertise?

c Is the source sufficiently up to date?

d What claims – if any – does it make? Are these claims backed up by evidence or reasoning? Can we verify any facts? Why do you think this source has been written?

e Does it present a local, national or global perspective?

Activity: Developing your log

Name: Anita				
Date/time and place	Task	Source (where relevant)	My notes	Action?
05/06/22 At home	Did web-search to find out more on 'fast fashion'	United Nations movement www. unfashionalliance.org website	• Grid gives factual info on clothing industry as a whole	

6 The log above is only partly complete.

a Copy and complete it, adding information about where the source comes from, when it was produced, plus anything that might suggest a particular perspective.

b You could also suggest any further steps you need to take. For example, does this source provide enough information about the UN perspective?

Apply

Final task

Read this extract from an interview in a popular fashion magazine, *Modo*. The interview is with the managing director of a major international fashion brand.

> Some people use the term 'fast fashion' to describe our business selling clothes globally. I get angry about this. Yes, I admit we produce clothing which we sell cheaply but 'fast' doesn't mean poor quality. No, we're fast because our employees are hard workers, because our **supply chains** are efficient, and because our customers always want the **next big thing** in fashion. They don't want to wait.
>
> Leon Smith, MD, Flash Fash Ltd
>
> *Modo* magazine, 19th September 2015

7 Using a log like the one above, record your thoughts on this source.

Note down:

a when you read this source (and whether you were working independently at home or in class)

b where the source comes from and how up to date it is

c how reliable a statement it is of the brand's perspective

d what the perspective (if any) of the author is.

Vocabulary

supply chains: links between factory, transport and shop

next big thing: a new popular trend or idea

Reflective plenary

8 How has your thinking changed – if at all – on the issue as the unit has progressed? Write a summative statement which you could add to your log explaining your thought processes. Use these prompts.

At the start, I believed that…

However, now… because…

Generating ideas and structuring a response

Skills focus

✓ Research, reflection, evaluation, analysis, communication

Objective

- To use different approaches to generate ideas
- To organise ideas into a structure for a response

How do I plan a written response?

If you are setting out to answer a question on a global issue, it is important to plan for the range of perspectives you might need to reference. To do this, you can follow a clear set of steps.

One way in which you can start to answer a question is to **annotate** it. Imagine you are trying to answer this question:

Key terms

annotate: to add notes around a text

question stem – asking you: 'What are the ways?'

specific focus – on the art of persuasion

How do fashion companies persuade consumers to buy the latest trends?

broad topic area

These annotations break down the question into what it is *you* have to do (in this case, it's an explanatory task rather than one asking for your opinion), and what the broad and specific focuses are.

Starting point

1 a Copy and annotate this question in the same way as the example above.
Should the global fashion industry change the way it operates?

b How is this question different from the first question in what it is asking you to do? (Look at the word 'Should'.)

c How are the general and specific focuses different?

Explore

The question is an investigative one, requiring you to reach a conclusion. But, by itself, the annotations will not be sufficient to structure an essay response.

So, here are two possible approaches.

Approach 1: 'Exploding' the issue

You could list or generate ideas around the key issue of the way the fashion industry operates. For example, who might have a perspective on this?

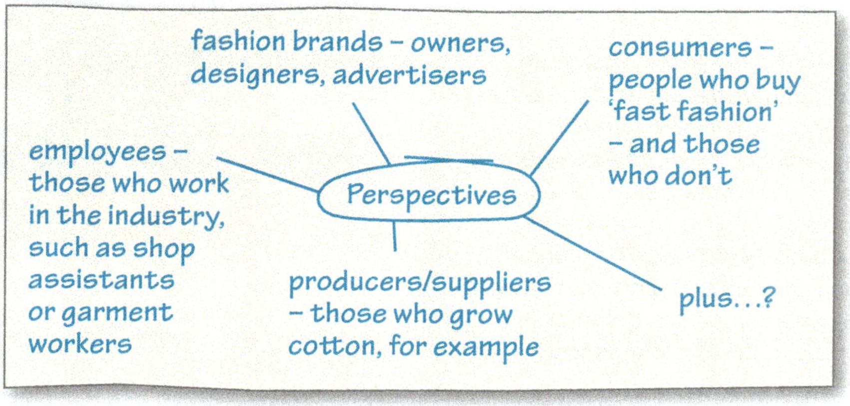

Approach 2: Using topics as lenses

Another way would be to use different 'lenses' or windows to explore the issue. These would not be perspectives as such but different angles through which you could look at the issue.

employment	poverty and inequality
environment, pollution and conservation	globalisation

Activity: Linking from plan to sources

Think back to the picture of the discarded clothes in Unit 2.4.1. Your research has uncovered that the image has been used as part of a poster from **Friends of the Earth** criticising 'fast fashion' because of the amount of waste it generates. Using both the 'perspectives' and 'lens' approaches, you note down the following ideas.

Perspectives: consumers, **pressure groups**

Lenses: environment, pollution, conservation, poverty and inequality

2 Look back at the other two sources from Unit 2.4.1 (the UN webpage with data; the interview in *Modo* magazine).
   a Which, if any, of the groups listed in Approach 1 are represented in each source?
   b Which, if any, of the 'lenses' in Approach 2 would be an appropriate way to explore the sources?
3 Which of the groups in Approach 1 and the lenses in Approach 2 are not 'covered' by these sources and would need further investigation?

Vocabulary

Friends of the Earth: an environmental pressure group

pressure groups: organised groups who work to persuade organisations and governments to change policies or laws

You can use Approach 1 or 2 to expand your understanding of the issue. For example, while the UN source made general references to reducing the 'environmental and social' impact, and backed that up with some data about waste, it didn't tell you anything about the workers' perspective, pay or employment rights.

Read this extract from an **autobiography** of reporter Lia Davis.

One of my first reporting jobs was working **undercover** as a **home-worker** earning 15 cents an hour to add the finishing touches to garments such as buttons and embroidery. I met others, also working at home, including extremely poor women, some aged 17 or under. I even saw a child of about 10 or 11 doing this work. The workers I spoke to rarely had an employment contract, and many suffered **chronic** illnesses such as back pain and worsening eyesight. They were often paid late – and sometimes not at all – if they didn't meet the very high number of items demanded by the supplier.

When I questioned some of the big brands about this, they told me they had taken steps to improve factory working but admitted they had not addressed the home-working issue. Their response was that often the factory did not tell them it **sub-contracted** the process to companies with lots of home-workers.

Of course, such work did provide vital employment for women and girls who might not have any alternative form of income. In this respect, improving conditions rather than banning such work altogether is a better solution.

Lia Davis, *A Reporting Life* (published 2021, BigLife Books)

Vocabulary

autobiography: book about your own life

undercover: hiding your real identity

home-worker: someone who does a job based in their own home

chronic: persistent or returning

sub-contracted: when a business pays another one to do work on its behalf

Activity: Evaluating the source

4 Write brief notes in response to these questions.

a Is it going to help me answer the essay question? (Look at the final paragraph.)

b Who has produced this source? What is the writer's expertise?

c Is it sufficiently up to date?

d What claims – if any – does it make? Are these claims backed up by evidence or reasoning? Can we verify any facts?

e Why has it been written?

f What is the writer's viewpoint or perspective on the issue?

Develop

Now look at the way one student has used this source – and the topics and sources mentioned earlier – to develop an essay plan.

Should the global fashion industry change the way it operates? (Write 750–800 words)

Section 1: Introduction (75 words)

- A brief explanation of the title.
- Will touch on some of the key issues – considering causes of the issue and introducing consequences
- Mention my own perspective and understanding at start of the research process.

Section 2: Globalisation (150–175 words)

- Could explore benefits and problems of global fashion industry.
- Use some of the statistics/data about the clothing industry from the UN web source as context.
- Use the article from the Modo director.

Section 3: Environment, pollution and conservation (150–175 words)

- Explore the impact of the global fashion industry on the environment.
- Use the picture of dumped clothes or similar to illustrate.
- Draw on other sources (the UN website mentions amount of waste in the textile industry).

Activity: Thinking ahead

5 Now complete the remainder of the plan. Add two further sections using the headings below.

Section 4: Poverty and wealth inequality – and employment (150–175 words)

- This could explore different perspectives on...
- This could draw on the following sources...

Section 5: Technology, industry and innovation (150–175 words)

- This could explore how technology could...
- This could draw on sources such as...

Section 6: Conclusion (75–100 words)

This should draw together your findings and sum up the key arguments for or against the question in the essay title.

Activity: Reflecting on your writing

6 This is not the only way you could structure your writing. Work in pairs to discuss how else you could organise it. Would there be any benefit in prioritising particular arguments?

Apply

Final task

7 In the course of your research, you have identified the following additional sources. Where might you refer to these in the plan above?

- **a** an interview with a trade unionist who represents workers in the garment industry
- **b** an article from a campaign group about the impact of chemical dyes on river systems
- **c** data on the prevalence of child labour in different sectors
- **d** data showing typical prices for basic garments in some popular fashion stores

Reflective plenary

8 In the essay plan above, where would there be opportunities to draw on local or national perspectives? For example, are there people you know locally who are employed in the fashion or textile industry? What big brand shops do you have access to where you live?

Using sources and citing references in an argument

Skills focus
✓ Research, communication

Objective
- To cite sources accurately to support an argument
- To quote or paraphrase fluently

How do I make sure I refer to sources correctly, while conveying my point of view?

Engaging with sources will be a key part of developing your argument and can lend authority to what you say. How you refer to them and the use you make of them are important skills to practise and develop. It is especially important that you use **references** and do not pass off the words that others say or write as your own.

Key terms

references: citation or quotation of a source of information reproduced in a report

Starting point

1 Imagine you complete some difficult mathematics homework. The next day, a friend borrows your homework book and copies your answers. The teacher compliments your friend on how well they have answered the question. Discuss this situation in pairs.

a Is there anything wrong with this?

b How would it make you feel?

Explore

When you write an argument in an essay or research report, you will **cite** other people's work, including:

- information or ideas a source made you aware of
- information or perspectives provided by others which help support the argument you wish to make.

To cite properly, you can **quote** a source directly – or **paraphrase** what it says. In both cases, you must **acknowledge** the source.

Quote directly	Paraphrase
Although Davis (2021) describes how home-working on garments provides 'vital employment' for many women, she stresses how conditions remain very poor (p.5).	*Despite the fact that Davis (2021) describes how home-working on garments keeps many women in valuable work, she stresses how conditions remain very poor.*

Key terms

cite: to refer to

quote: when you include the actual words someone says or writes in your own work

paraphrase: when you express what someone says in your own words

acknowledge: recognise or make clear

Activity: Communicating other people's ideas

2 Discuss the following in pairs.

a Which words in the table above have been quoted directly from Davis? How do you know?

b What alternative wording is used in the right-hand column to provide the same information?

Whether you are writing about fast fashion or space exploration, you should stick to some basic **conventions** when using citations. These include:

- the name of the author/organisation quoted
- the date of the source from which the idea/information or quotation comes
- a page number.

There are a number of different approaches to citation, but you should use one system consistently. In the following system, there is a brief reference to the author, date and page number in the main body of the essay. This is supported with a **bibliography** that should come at the end of your essay.

In your essay, a reference would follow this formula:

> Davis (2021) describes how home-working on garments provides 'vital employment' for many women, even though conditions remain very poor (p.5).

The bibliography provides details of all the sources cited in your essay in an alphabetical list:

> Ahmed, A. (1999). On the Front Line of Fashion. *India Today*, 11. 51–68
>
> Davis, L. (2021). *A Reporting Life*. New York: Big Life Books.
>
> United Nations Fashion Alliance (2022). The Clothing and textile industry today. United Nations Fashion Alliance. Available at: *https://www.unfashionalliance.org* [Accessed 5 June 2022].

Key terms

conventions: accepted way of doing things

bibliography: list of works or sources referred to in the main text (usually comes at the end of the essay)

Activity: Practising reference skills

The following paragraph comes from one student's essay based on the plan in Unit 2.4.2. He is using the UN webpage information from Unit 2.4.1 to support an argument that fast fashion should be reduced.

> I have learned about the damage the fashion industry does to the ecosystem. Major organisations have highlighted the environmental damage directly caused by the textile industry, for example in the 9% of annual micro-plastic losses to the oceans.

3 Look again at the log on page 83 of Unit 2.4.1. Rewrite the sentence above to ensure the source is cited properly. There will be a bibliography at the end of the essay, so for now all you need to include is:

- quotation marks around the words directly taken from the source
- clear reference to the author or organisation, with full details given in the bibliography.

Language support

When you paraphrase, you take the general meaning of a text and put it into your own words. Sometimes, simple synonyms can help. For example:

'vital employment' → valuable work

Develop

When you use other people's ideas or research, you need to be very careful not to pass them off as your own. Presenting other people's work as your own is called plagiarism.

Activity: Reflecting on key issues

4 Discuss with a partner why you should avoid plagiarism.

a What would happen if your plagiarism was discovered by a teacher or examiner?

b What (negative) impact would *not* citing your sources have on your argument as a whole?

Here, a student has plagiarised one of the sources from Units 2.4.1 and 2.4.2.

> I am outraged at bad employment practices where I have seen the chronic illnesses suffered by home-workers such as back pain and worsening eyesight.

Activity: Identifying plagiarism

5 In pairs, identify and discuss:

a Which source has been plagiarised?

b In what way?

Apply

Now read this article about the environmental impacts of the fashion industry.

Is fashion bad for the environment?

By Morgan McFall-Johnsen, 31st January 2020

Is fashion bad for the environment? | World Economic Forum (weforum.org)

It takes about 700 gallons of water to produce one cotton shirt. That's enough water for one person to drink at least eight cups per day for three-and-a-half years. It takes about 2,000 gallons of water to produce a pair of jeans. That's more than enough for one person to drink eight cups per day for 10 years. That's because both the jeans and the shirt are made from a highly water-intensive plant: cotton.

In Uzbekistan, for example, cotton farming used up so much water from the Aral Sea that it dried up after about 50 years. Once one of the world's four largest lakes, the Aral Sea is now little more than desert and a few small ponds.

Final task

6 Complete a log entry for this source, using the format from Unit 2.4.1. Remember to include details about the perspective, any questions it raises, who produced the source, and so on.

7 When you have finished, rewrite the following paragraph, citing the source in the most appropriate place and using the conventions you have learned about. Add a bibliography.

> A further problem with regard to the environment is the huge water consumption required to make many materials. Cotton, for example, according to some observers, uses up to 700 gallons just to produce one shirt. This is clearly unsustainable.

Reflective plenary

8 Look back over notes you have made on any sources that you have accessed as part of your investigation. Have you noted down sufficient details to cite them correctly? If not, go back to the source and add what is needed.

Language support

Use phrases such as 'according to', 'as stated in', 'as reported in' when quoting or citing sources.

Applying what you have learned

How do I bring together arguments, evidence and references in a written response?

Skills focus

✓ Research, analysis, evaluation, communication, reflection

Objective

- To make notes on a new source and reflect on its impact
- To write a response to a question setting out reasons and evidence for a choice

Starting point

1 In a small group, share what you have collectively learned about the fashion and textile industry so far. Where do you currently stand on the question: *Should the global fashion industry change the way it operates?*

Explore

One member of your group has identified this further source. You have discussed it and begun to annotate it.

Sustainability is the new goal for the fashion industry

By Ryan Werner

Business For Business magazine, 9th May 2022

For far too long, fashion companies have been in the firing line of environmental activists. They have been quick to point out that denim requires an enormous amount of water just to make one pair of jeans. For this reason, Levi's latest collection, Water<Less, is a fantastic example of one company's commitment to sustainability. Levi's claim that the collection uses up to 96% less water. That is amazing. They also say they're promoting sustainability across the whole design and manufacturing process and are aiming for cotton that is 100% sustainably sourced. They're even looking at recycling old jeans for home insulation.

positive step but just one company

What does this mean in practice?

this is a goal

What about other brands? Well, H&M is rejecting its old fast-fashion ethos with its new Conscious collection. This is made up of organic cotton and recycled polyester. And if you're a shopper, you can even recycle your unwanted clothes at their stores in return for a discount on future purchases. It's a win-win. Put that alongside the company's goal to use only sustainably sourced materials by 2030 and you have a business that's putting the environment first.

It's brilliant to see the fashion industry finally getting serious about sustainability.

Activity: Exploring the text

2 a Make your own notes on the second paragraph and record key details about the source in your log.

b Use your usual process for checking the text itself (date, relevance, purpose, etc.), claims the writer makes, their expertise, any facts they include, and so on.

c Note down any ways in which the source enables you to answer the question about how the fashion industry operates.

d Briefly, check back to the plan set out in Unit 2.4.2. Where might this source fit if included in a longer essay-style response?

Activity: Honing the plan

3 Using the plan from Unit 2.4.2, make any further notes related to the fashion industry, and decide what your viewpoint is with regard to the essay question. If it helps you to decide, create a quick table of 'reasons for' and 'reasons against' like the one below.

Reasons to change the way the industry operates	Reasons not to
Poor working conditions of some employees	*Garment work gives much needed employment to women*

Develop

How could you refer to this source in an effective way in your writing? You have already learned how to cite a source, but how can you use it to support your own perspective?

Look at how one student has approached it.

> Whilst it is easy to blame fashion companies for acting too slowly on 'fast fashion', some of the big brands say they are committed to change. For example, Levi's claim their latest collection 'Water<Less' consumes up to 96% less water than other products of theirs (R. Werner, 2020). Although this may appear to be positive, it is only one of many collections that Levi's sells.

first clause of sentence introduces the counter-argument

second clause introduces alternative perspective

evidence cited by paraphrasing source

final sentence questions how significant claim is, showing writer's perspective

Activity: Citing a source to support an argument

4 The same student now wants to question H&M's idea of people returning unwanted clothes. Using a similar model to the one above, complete her next paragraph.

Checklist for success

- ✔ Either quote from or paraphrase the relevant section from the article. (See Unit 2.4.3 pages 88–89 for details about how to quote directly using speech marks or to paraphrase using your own words.)
- ✔ Cite the source accurately: simply copy the example above if you are paraphrasing or add more detail, such as the page number, if you are quoting directly. Add a bibliographical entry.
- ✔ Draw a conclusion from the information H&M has given, using these prompts:
  The article seems to support the idea that other companies also claim to have innovative ideas about cutting waste. For example, H&M…
  Whilst this appears to be positive…

Language support

You can use words such as 'claim', 'suggest' or 'appears to be' to question the validity of an argument or statement. In the article itself, notice how the writer uses these terms on some occasions, and on others, takes the companies' claims at face value.

Apply

Final task

5 Write the opening two sections (up to 250 words) of an essay in response to the question: *Should the global fashion industry change the way it operates?*

a Begin with an introduction, setting the context and explaining the background to the issue.

b Choose any of the lenses or angles from the plan that you would most like to write about and make it the focus of the second section you write.

Checklist for success

- ✔ Make your own perspective clear – 'should' or 'should not' – and provide evidence for it.
- ✔ Refer to any of the sources from this chapter or any others you have identified in your own research.
- ✔ Evaluate the different arguments and perspectives presented by your sources.
- ✔ Cite any sources you refer to and include a brief bibliography at the end of your 250 words.

Reflective plenary

6 When you have completed your short essay responses, share the final drafts with a partner or within a small group. What is your perspective now on the fashion industry? Why? Write up your final reflections on the issue – perhaps in your log.

Language support

Use linking phrases such as 'so', 'because', 'for this reason', 'as the author suggests', 'in this way', 'therefore' to give evidence in support of your point.

Check your progress

By the end of this chapter, you should have learned how to:

- create useful notes which record the thinking you have done, the sources you have accessed, and the next steps you need to take
- generate ideas from different perspectives and plan a structure for an extended written response
- quote, cite and paraphrase sources accurately and usefully
- write fluently and persuasively about sources for a longer, written response.

Next steps

- Research the issue of fast fashion further and challenge yourself to find a global perspective that presents a positive argument about it. You could also see if you can find out further facts or data about fashion companies' plans to improve their environmental impact.

- What else has caught your interest in this chapter? Were you inspired to explore the fashion and textile industry more widely or perhaps to find out about careers within it? Has your research changed the way you think about the clothes you wear and buy? Make a note of one to two ideas or interests you'd like to take further, and how you would go about doing this.

Section 3: Developing skills for the written exam

3

In this section, you will continue to build your analytical and evaluative skills. You will be provided with a range of source texts around a particular issue, and you will look at the evidence these sources provide and how effectively they argue for the perspectives they present. You will test the claims they make, then use your understanding of the issue and the sources to argue for a course of action to help to improve or solve the problem.

You will be provided with two sets of source texts: one on the topic of 'Education for all'; and one on the topic of 'Climate change, energy and resources'.

Example answers to practice questions have been included throughout the chapter for you to assess, learn from and improve. These answers have been written by our authors.

You will be developing the following skills:

3.0 Reading sources

3.1 Identifying and explaining information

3.2 Describing a perspective

3.3 Justifying opinions with reasoning and evidence

3.4 Investigating the strengths and weaknesses of research

3.5 Testing a claim

3.6 Evaluating arguments

3.7 Developing lines of reasoning to support a course of action 1

3.8 Developing lines of reasoning to support a course of action 2.

Reading sources

Education sources

These are the sources you'll use for the topic: Education for all.

Source 1

The United Nations has a sustainable development goal that by 2030 all girls and boys should be able to complete free, quality primary and secondary education. This is in the interests of global equality. According to **UNESCO**, in 2018, 59 million children of primary school age were receiving no formal education. This means that their choices about their futures were seriously limited.

Governments need to evaluate the impact of education on economic development. Education is expensive to provide, and governments need to know that it provides good value. The United Nations supplies information to help countries to make good decisions. This source is a chart showing how education related to national wealth. It is based on UN data.

This graph shows four patterns of educational provision and the relative wealth of countries implementing those patterns.

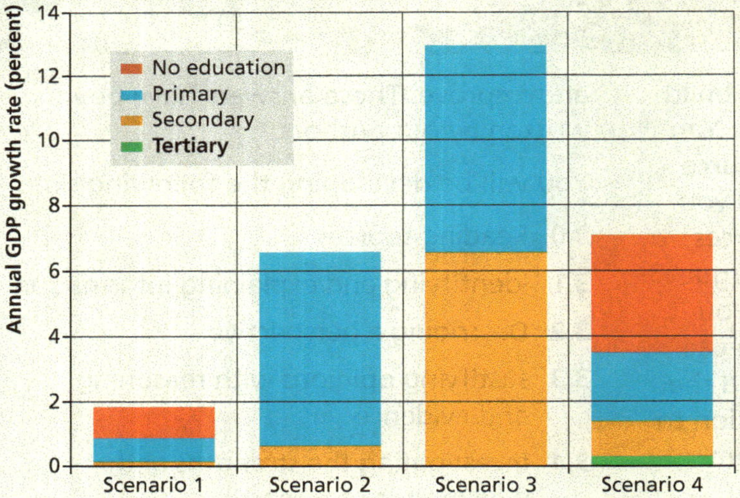

From *Economic Growth in Developing Countries: Education Proves Key, IIASA 2008*

Vocabulary

UNESCO: the United Nations Educational, Scientific and Cultural Organization

GDP: or **Gross Domestic Product**, indicates a country's wealth from the goods and services it produces and provides

tertiary: college or university education

Source 2

Schools are often judged on the basis of their exam results. I have children of my own and I know just how important statistics on school exam results can be.

However, I own restaurants and I know that none of those statistics tell the whole story of children's education, and do not reflect the personal skills children gain through their time at school.

As a restaurant owner, I need to be able to employ adults who leave education with the ability to work in a team. They need to be able to listen to what others have to say, and to contribute ideas without objecting if others don't agree with them. What's more, young people need to be able to explain their ideas if they believe that they are right.

I need workers who can be flexible, who are able to move between teams. Useful workers can solve straightforward problems, and don't forever turn to a superior for answers. I need a workforce that can carry out tasks without constantly needing to be told what comes next.

I cannot teach all these skills when young people come to me for a job. Their schools have a role in preparing them for life. Primary schools have children working through problems of all sorts in teams, offering their ideas in many different ways. Can secondary schools take on a greater role in further developing these skills to produce workers who are ready for the workplace?

Extract from a feature about education written by a restaurant owner

Source 3

A school student's research project

I wanted to find out about the purpose of education in today's world for our team project. To make a start, and taking notebook and pen, I decided to ask my teachers what they thought. This seemed a sensible start as they are experts, even though they may have a vested interest in the subject.

My head teacher said that it was about learning how to learn. Most teachers understand that teaching is about giving students the skills that they need for the future. Today's learners will be in a world of change, so facts matter less.

My Information Technology teacher said IT was about knowing how to find out information safely, and to recognise the threats of online communications.

My Engineering teacher said that engineering is all about problem-solving, and that the world needs problem-solvers to make national economies stronger. She said that Engineering brings together the skills of maths and science.

My form teacher said that education needs to make you able to take care of yourself, to look after yourself and know about foods and cooking as well as everything else.

From a school research project

Source 4

A radio discussion about business and education

Edie and Pablo were heard in a radio discussion about how learners are taught about the world of business.

Edie

I have wanted to work in the world of fashion since I was young, so I would like to develop skills that will enable me to manage a fashion business. The fashion industry is really important internationally, and contributes to the national wealth of countries where clothes are made and sold.

How can I find out what the fashion industry does?

My Business Studies teacher in school is a really good teacher and his classes always get good exam results. We have analysed case studies from different types of businesses: from mining, to market stalls and from the creative industries.

He has taught me about how businesses have sections with different functions: Finance, Administration, Design and Development being some of them in the creative industries. You must be good at maths to work in the finance department. I am good at art and design, so would suit a job designing fashion.

I have every confidence that I will achieve what I want to.

Pablo

I have wanted to own a business since I was young. Where I live there are all sorts of businesses. I take Business as a subject at school, but I can't say I enjoy learning from books.

Our school has a link with a local pottery manufacturer. Today we were introduced to the factory through a virtual tour. We saw what happens at the Reception desk. We went to the stores department to learn how **just in time ordering** is put into action and we were taught about how this saves money for the business. We went to the finance department and saw how software systems are used to do ordering and invoicing. We went to the pottery and saw how manufacturing software runs the processes that make cups and plates.

It has been agreed that I can do a work placement in the stores during my holiday. They will even pay me. I am excited about this because I will learn some practical skills that I will need to start my own business in the future. The pottery may even offer me a job when I leave school, if I do well while I am working there.

Vocabulary

just in time ordering: when a business buys materials for production at the time they are needed, instead of buying and storing materials for future use

Climate change sources

These are the sources you'll use for the topic: Climate change, energy and resources.

Source 5

COP26 saw Glasgow filled with people from all over the world who supported the United Nations' aims of limiting climate change.

Climate change has already reduced access to clean water in some countries. One in three people worldwide has no access to safe, clean drinking water. The sustainable goals that will limit climate change include using less gas and coal as fuel, and cutting down fewer trees, as these reduce the amount of carbon dioxide in the air.

The United Nations provides information that helps us to play our part in developing a sustainable world, such as this graphic that offers guidance for everyone:

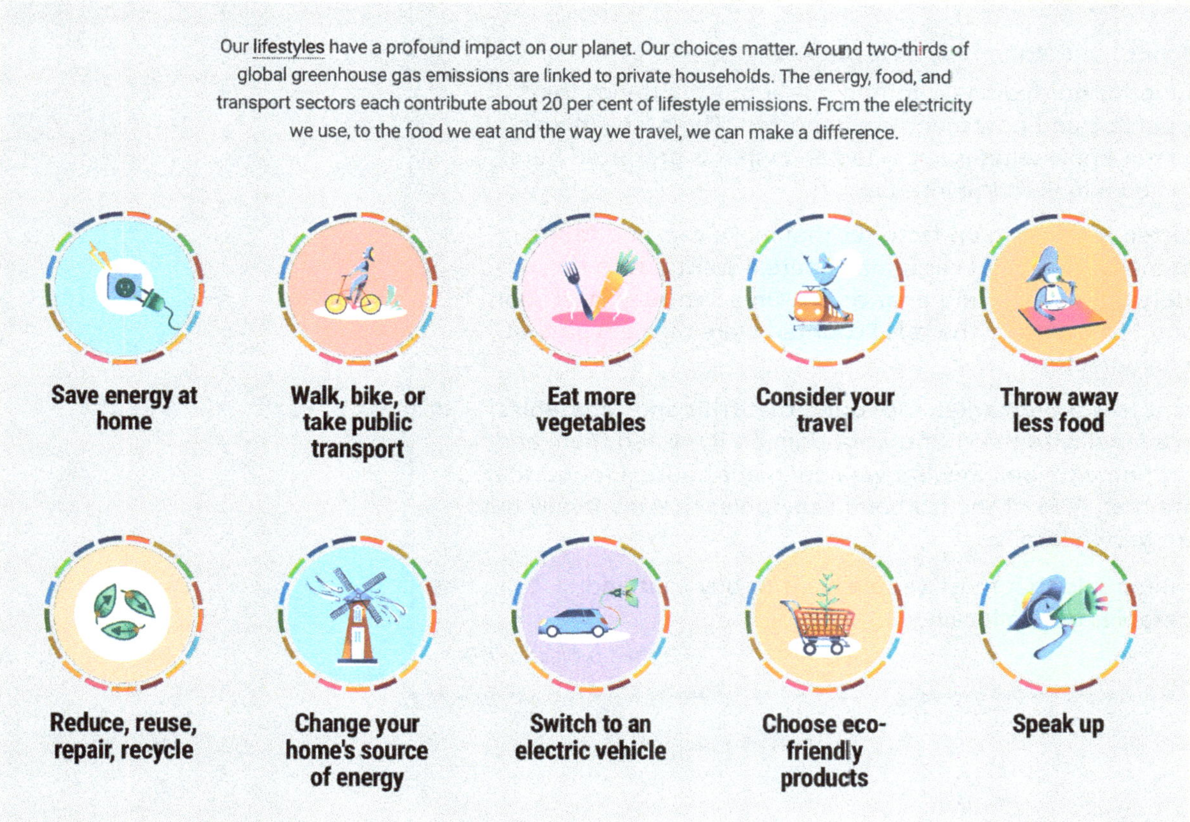

From the United Nations Act Now website, accessed 16/01/2022

Vocabulary

COP26: UN Climate Change Conference, held in the Scottish city of Glasgow

Source 6

Germany gets it right

Germany has used **biomass technology** to produce energy for at least forty years. However, new developments have meant that a powerplant fuelled only by biomass has been used to provide all the energy needs of a fairly large town in Germany. This will mean that less polluting gas will be released into the atmosphere in that region.

This sounds like great news and provides an excellent model for other cities to follow. If this happens, other countries that use coal and gas to fuel power stations will reduce the extent to which they contribute to global warming.

Heard during a radio programme

Vocabulary

biomass technology: use of unwanted organic materials, such as food waste, instead of coal and gas to generate electricity

Source 7

A school student's research project

My job for our team was to find out about the things that people buy and how many are imported. The problem was, I did not know what is imported and what is produced here. So, I had a look at the internet.

I started by looking up factories that make cars and found that only one type of car is made here. I went out to the middle of town and did a car count. On a Saturday afternoon I found that 10% of the cars I counted were of the type that we manufacture.

I went to a supermarket and found that fruit and vegetables had a label with the country of origin on it. I listed them and went home to look at what we had in our house. I found that more than 50% of the fruit and vegetables that my family buys were grown locally.

My mum said that most people want to buy fruit and vegetables grown locally.

From a project, 2019

Source 8

A school debate about the value of air travel

Serena

'The house proposes that air travel is vital to our wellbeing. There are students in this class whose families live overseas. It is impossible to imagine only being able to see them once a year, as would be true without air travel. We need to be able to fly! Who has time to travel across the world by ship? Not us!

I live in a small country that cannot provide all the food that we need. How poor would life be if we could only have fruits that we could grow here? Imagine, no kiwi fruits, no strawberries or blueberries. And it is not only fruits we would have to do without. Think of the vegetables we could not have for more than half of the year. Wouldn't eating be boring?

Air freight is the quickest way of getting perishables to us – and of getting us home for holidays. Leave air travel alone.'

Qazi

'Air travel is killing our world. When an aircraft takes off it burns fuel, and **particulate matter** from the emissions are released into the air, along with carbon dioxide. This does huge damage to the atmosphere. Particulate pollution stops our lungs working properly, and makes it harder for us to get oxygen – just look how many of us suffer from asthma.

The metals used in the construction of aircraft and their engines are made using electricity from coal and gas. Extracting these fuels again releases particulates and carbon dioxide into the air. Slowly we are poisoning our world. It is not as though air travel is essential – all industries do some damage to the world, but some we need, such as brickmaking for building materials for our homes. We should remove industries that we do not need.'

Vocabulary

particulate matter: tiny solid or liquid particles found in the air, especially those produced when fuel is burned

Identifying and explaining information

Skills focus
✓ Researching, analysing and evaluating information

Objective
- To locate and select information from sources
- To explain reasons for your answers

How can I identify and explain information from sources?

Starting point

1 In pairs discuss: What is a fact? Do facts always remain the same? Why – or why not?

When you are studying a topic for Global Perspectives, you will often be given data sources like graphs or tables, and be asked to extract information from them, and explain what they show.

Explore

You are going to be looking at a source that will provide information about the relationship between education and a country's wealth. When you first read a source, you need to look at all parts of it carefully.

- Look at what the heading shows the chart or graph to be about.
- Study the axes to work out what the pattern shows.
- Remember to read all the information around the chart or graph as every part of what you are given will be important when you look for answers to questions.

Activity: Reading and understanding a statistical source

Look at the graph from Source 1 on page 98.

2 a Which part of the source gives you a measure of national wealth?

b Which part of the source gives you patterns of educational provision?

c What does the light blue shading mean?

Activity: Interpreting a data source

3 Now look more closely. Work with a partner to answer these questions. For each question, record which part(s) of the source gives you the necessary information.
   - a What is this source about?
   - b What measure of national wealth is used?
   - c What does the red area show?
   - d Which scenario of educational provision leads to the lowest annual GDP rates?
   - e What is the difference between scenarios 2 and 4?
   - f What is the difference between scenarios 2 and 3?
   - g What does the source tell you about how important primary education is?
   - h What does the source tell you about how important secondary education is?

Develop

Now you've studied the source thoroughly, look at these practice questions.

Questions on a source may ask for one detail or one **fact**. Or they may ask you to compare two elements in the data. Take care to check what you are being asked to do. You might be asked to identify elements such as an **opinion**, an example of **bias** or **vested interest**, a **prediction** or a **value judgment**.

Practice questions

1 Study Source 1 on page 98.

(a) According to Source 1, how many children of primary age were not receiving formal education in 2018? [1]

(b) (i) Identify a fact that is given about the United Nations. [1]

(b) (ii) Explain why the example you have given is a fact. [2]

It is important to read the question stems carefully in short answer questions, to find out what you are being asked for. For example:

<u>According to Source 1</u> means that you should not give your own opinion here.

<u>Identify</u> means that you should just find and state a piece of information, in this case a fact, from the source.

<u>Explain why</u> asks you to give reasons for your answer.

Activity: Answering questions with clarity

4 Identify the question stems in the practice questions above. Then try answering the questions yourself.

Key terms

fact: something that is known or can be proved to be true

opinion: a view or judgement formed about something, not based on fact or knowledge

bias: unfairly prejudiced for or against something or someone (for example, in Source 8, Serena wants to visit family overseas during holidays and this colours her view of the damage done by aircraft)

vested interest: a personal reason for involvement in an undertaking or situation, especially expecting financial or some other gain (for example, in Source 4, Pablo praises a visit to the factory that has offered him a job)

prediction: what someone thinks will happen in the future (for example, in Source 4, Edie says she 'would suit a job designing fashion')

value judgement: an assessment of something as good or bad in terms of someone's standards or priorities (for example, in Source 4, Edie says, 'My Business Studies teacher in school is a really good teacher')

Activity: Analysing answers

Complete activities 4 and 5 first working independently, then sharing in pairs, then groups, refining your explanations as you hear from others.

5 **a** Which of the following sample answers to **practice question (b) (i)** on the previous page do you think is better? Suggest reasons why.

Answer 1: A fact in Source 1 is that the UN has sustainability goals.

Answer 2: *A fact is the United Nations has a sustainable development goal for equal access globally to primary and secondary education by 2030.*

b Which of the following sample answers to **practice question (b) (ii)** on the previous page do you think is better? You are looking for an answer that explains what a fact is, using the example the student gave.

Answer 1: This is a fact because I know it is what the UN aims for.

Answer 2: *This is a fact because you can check online that the UN has sustainability goals about access to primary and secondary education. You can also check the target date, that equal access should be achieved by 2030.*

Apply

Working with sources from the topic: Climate change, energy and resources

Now that you have analysed a statistical source on the topic of Education for all, you will be able to apply your skills to a different set of sources. This time, you'll be looking at the topic of Climate change, energy and resources.

Final task

Identifying and explaining information from different sources

6 Go to Sources 5 and 6 on pages 101–103. Source 5 is concerned with COP26 and UN guidance on how everyone can play their part in developing a sustainable world. Source 6 is about providing power for homes using biomass technology.

Read the sources fully before you answer these practice questions.

Practice questions

1 Study Sources 5 and 6.

(a) According to Source 5, what proportion of people worldwide have no access to safe, clean drinking water? [1]

(b) (i) Identify **one** example of a prediction from Source 6. [1]

(b) (ii) Explain why the example you identified is a prediction. [2]

Reflective plenary

7 In pairs, discuss whether you found it difficult to avoid giving your own views in response to the practice questions in this unit.

Describing a perspective

Skills focus

✓ Researching, analysing and evaluating information

Objective

- To identify, analyse and describe a perspective

How can I describe a perspective?

Starting point

1 a In pairs, look at this picture and discuss what you think it might suggest about education. Who is in the picture? How is the learning taking place? What do you think the girls are studying? What is the role of the learner? Is there an overall message the picture gives you?

b What is your viewpoint on these ideas?

If you explain your viewpoint, support it with reasons and provide evidence, your viewpoint becomes a **perspective**.

In this unit, you will be focusing on describing perspectives that you identify in various sources. (See Section 2, Unit 1 if you need a reminder.)

Explore

You are going to be looking at Source 2 on page 99 in some detail, to identify, **analyse** and **describe** the writer's perspective on the purpose of education.

When you're describing perspective from a source, you need to describe its elements:

- identify the **issue**
- identify the causes of the issue
- identify consequences of the issue

Key terms

perspective: a viewpoint on an issue based on evidence and reasoning

analyse: examine in detail to show meaning, identify elements and the relationship between them

describe: state the main points, characteristics and features

issue: an important subject or problem for discussion

- identify the values of the writer or speaker
- identify actions that are recommended
- identify the **evidence** and reasoning that would support that perspective.

Let's start by looking at the speech below.

> Fewer than 10% of our best female brains are taking on advanced level study in science, technology, engineering and maths. When asked why, most considered these subjects to be hard and boring. Partly it may also be because careers in science and engineering are not glamorous and are male-dominated. This has meant that many of our most able are not focused on the careers that make other countries wealthy. What can be done about it? We must ensure that the resources and equipment used in our schools for teaching maths, science, technology and engineering are up-to-date and that girls actually use them. We must also ensure girls are introduced to female role models in STEM careers.

Key terms

evidence: information about a global issue that helps to develop understanding or prove that something is true or false

Describing a perspective by identifying its elements:

Describing the perspective	
Elements of the perspective	
the issue	that the most able girls are not choosing to study maths, science, technology and engineering
two causes are found	the girls asked find maths and science hard and boring in school; STEM careers are not seen as glamorous and jobs are usually done by men
there is one consequence	able girls not going into those careers damages the country's economic potential
three actions are suggested	put up-to-date equipment into schools; make sure girls use the equipment and resources; give girls female role models in STEM jobs
the values of the speaker	that STEM careers are suitable for all capable young people
evidence used	statistics; opinions of girls
reasoning used	changing how subjects are taught can make more able girls want to study maths, science, technology and engineering, and this will help to make our country wealthy

Activity: Planning to describe a perspective

2 Read the practice question below.

> **Practice questions**
>
> **1** Study Source 2.
>
> **(c)** Using Source 2, describe the restaurant owner's perspective on education. [6]

Complete the table to identify elements of the perspective from Source 2 on page 99.

Describing a perspective	
Elements of the perspective	
the issue	
cause(s)	
consequence(s)	
actions suggested	
the values of the speaker	
evidence used	
reasoning used	

Activity: Describing a perspective

3 Now use your notes to answer the practice question. Think on your own, then discuss with your partner. Write your answer.

Develop

Activity: Reviewing descriptions

Have a look at this sample answer that Chyou, a student, wrote.

> The issue is that learners are not leaving school with the skills they need for work. This is caused by schools focusing on results. For the restaurant owner, the consequence is that he/she has to spend time, and therefore money, on staff training. He/she is suggesting that secondary schools build on the good work of primary schools in developing teamwork and problem-solving skills. However, he/she is mostly speaking as a restaurant owner, with some bias in his/her views. The evidence is from what he/she has to do to train staff, and is subjective. However, he/she does state that he/she understands schools' focus on exam results. He/she does reason that there may be space at school for these skills to be developed more.

4 With a partner, look at what the strengths of this sample answer are. Has Chyou identified all the elements of a perspective? With this new understanding, try improving your own answer.

Apply your skills to the topic: Climate change, energy and resources

Consider the second topic that we are covering, Climate change, energy and resources, and read this practice question.

Practice questions

1 Study Source 6.

(c) From Source 6, describe the speaker's perspective on how energy is produced. [6]

Final task

5 a Read Source 6 on page 102 carefully, picking out elements of a perspective and the evidence that helps you to describe it. Complete a grid like the one on page 110 to help you to identify elements of the perspective.

b Now write your response to the practice question.

Reflective plenary

6 Share your answer with a partner.

Have you:

- identified the elements of a perspective, as identified in the table?
- included phrases from the source to evidence your description?

Justifying opinions with reasoning and evidence

Skills focus
- ✓ Researching, analysing and evaluating information
- ✓ Developing and justifying a line of reasoning

Objective
- To identify elements of a perspective from a source
- To offer and justify your own opinions on it

How can I analyse arguments and evidence to justify my opinion?

Starting point

1 Discuss this question in pairs: Does it make any difference if one source was written by the UN and another source was written by a restaurant owner?

You will have opinions on many topics, from the purpose of education to whether you should buy fast fashion. While your opinions cannot be wrong, there is a difference between opinions that are just asserted without explanation or evidence, and those that are justified and supported. Understanding why opinions are held is important; explaining why they are held is even more important.

In this unit, you will be focusing on giving your opinion on perspectives presented in different sources. You will need to **explain** your opinion and justify it with relevant reasons.

Key terms

explain: say why you think this and support with relevant evidence

Explore

Read this practice question, which asks for you to explain your opinion.

Practice questions

1 Study Sources 1 and 2.

(d) Sources 1 and 2 suggest reasons why education is important. Which reason is the most important? Explain why. [8]

Activity: Checking on the evidence in preparation for answering a question

Read the sample practice question above and the planning grid below. You're going to be extracting key points from Sources 1 and 2 that provide opinions about the importance of education.

2 Work with a partner. Read the sources and complete the points in the table.

Source 1	Source 2
Education must be important because most systems include it	Education is important because it introduces problem-solving skills
	Education is important because it introduces…
Education is important because countries with the highest rates of GDP have compulsory education	Education is important because of the qualifications learners achieve
Education is important because the UN has a goal that…	Education is important because…

Develop

The next stage is to examine the arguments and evidence to arrive at your opinion as to which reason is the most important. There isn't a 'right answer'. What is important is that your opinion is clearly explained and justified, with evidence from the sources. It should be credible and clearly related to the issue.

Here is an example of one student's thought processes:

> **I think the most important reason is:** education improves the economy.
>
> **My justifications:** it has the greatest effect on the greatest number of people (Source 1), is measurable in its effects (Source 1); data supporting this is backed up by expert opinion (Source 2), so reliable.

Here, *one* reason why education is selected and the student's view that this is the most important reason is supported with a *good range of justifications*. This makes for a strong sample answer.

Here is another sample answer:

> *I think a most important reason is to bring equality to the world. I believe this because of what Source 1 shows me, that without access to education, children have limited choices about their futures. For nearly 60 million children in the world to face this in the 21st century is shocking. Source 2 supports this by showing how difficult it is to gain work without the skills education brings.*

Activity: Justifying reasons

3 One student has chosen the following reason as the most important for education:

I think that the most important reason for education is to give us the skills that matter throughout working life.

Work in pairs to identify a range of relevant justifications.

4 Now write your own answer to the practice question. State your opinion and provide a range of relevant justifications.

Apply

Now it is time to consider the second topic that we are covering, Climate change, energy and and resources. Read Sources 5 and 6 on pages 101–102 carefully, then look at the following practice question.

Practice questions

1 Study Sources 5 and 6.

(d) Sources 5 and 6 suggest actions that can reduce climate change. Which action do you think is most significant? [8]

Final task

5 Plan and answer the practice question.

Checklist for success

- ✔ Read both sources, noting the actions that aim to reduce climate change.
- ✔ Consider which of the actions you think is most significant in reducing climate change.
- ✔ List your justifications for thinking that this chosen action is most significant. You might want to consider factors such as:
  - how quickly change would come about
  - how much it would cost
  - how difficult it would be to make this a worldwide answer
  - how great an impact the change would have on climate change.
- ✔ Express your opinion, linking evidence from the sources to reasoning that explains why this is most significant to climate change.

Reflective plenary

6 Share your answer with a partner. Ask your partner to identify where you have:

- made it clear that you are explaining the significance of *one* action
- explain what the action is
- provided a range of relevant justifications for your opinion.

Investigating the strengths and weaknesses of research

Skills focus
✓ Researching, analysing and evaluating information

Objective
- To identify and explain the strengths and weaknesses of research

How do I evaluate the strengths and weaknesses of research?

Starting point

1 In pairs, consider this scenario.

You have been set a task at school. You have to find out about what people of different ages know and understand about the art of Rabindranath Tagore. You think your brother, who has some interest in art, will know so you ask him. His answer is that he thought Tagore was well known for his poems, not art. You write as an answer that 'even people interested in art do not know about Rabindranath Tagore's art'.

What problems are there with this piece of research?

Explore

When you are studying Global Perspectives, you may be asked to analyse and evaluate a piece of research, consider how effectively it has been conducted, and whether it achieves what it aimed to do.

Activity: Considering research methods that suit your aim

2 Read through the guidance below on conducting your own research. Think about how you could use this information to decide on a better way to conduct the research task about Tagore's art. Discuss in pairs what you would do.

Research methods

You can choose to carry out *primary research*, which means obtaining information that has not been available before. Methods include interviews, questionnaires and observation.

- In *interviews* the interviewer asks an interviewee a number of questions, often face-to-face or live. Interviews tend to be used with smaller groups to gather more in-depth information. There are two main types of interview: structured interviews and unstructured interviews.
- In *structured interviews* you use prepared questions that all interviewees answer in the same order. This makes analysis easier.
- *Unstructured interviews* are usually the least reliable from a research viewpoint, because no questions are prepared. Comparison of answers is difficult, making it harder to reach a conclusion. They might be useful early on in the process of research, to get a feel for an issue.
- A ***survey*** is a process that is used to collect information from a group of people. Sometimes, this chosen group will be given a **questionnaire** – a pre-determined set of questions that all participants respond to. The information is then analysed as a part of the survey.
- Sometimes you will want to conduct a survey using a *random sample* of people to avoid bias. On other occasions, you might want to use a *stratified sample* that will target particular groups. If you want to find out about different attitudes between 14-year-olds at your school, and people over 30, then those are the strata, or smaller groups, you could ask.
- If you want to know what a number of people think about the same question, then a survey is useful. If you survey a small number of people, you should make sure that your answers fit in with larger surveys by carrying out a check using online sources. This is called ***triangulating*** your results.

You can also choose to conduct *secondary research*, where you research from sources that already exist – from books, journals or online – to find information, perspectives and evidence on your subject of research.

Which research methods should you use? That depends on what you want to find out. If you want to know about a person's job or to investigate a question in detail, then you need to interview them. If you want to find out what a lot of people think, then a survey will be useful.

Key terms

survey: the process of collecting, analysing and interpreting data from a group of people

questionnaire: the term used to describe the set of questions you ask an individual

triangulating: using different data collection methods to check that your findings are correct

Develop

Read the annotated extract from Source 3 on page 99.

From Source 3: A school student's research project

I wanted to find out about the purpose of education in today's world for our team project. To make a start, and taking notebook and pen, I decided to ask my teachers what they thought. This seemed a sensible start as they are experts, even though they may have a vested interest in the subject.

My head teacher said that it was about learning how to learn. Most teachers understand that teaching is about giving students the skills that they need for the future. Today's learners will be in a world of change, so facts matter less.

[...]

My form teacher said that education needs to make you able to take care of yourself, to look after yourself and know about foods and cooking as well as everything else.

From a school research project

You are looking for a range of ages and interests in education. Is that what you see?

Experts in education – so are they appropriate to be included in the research?

Primary research. Is there evidence of the interview questions?

She has asked the head teacher, a person who could be expected to have a wider view of the purpose of education. Is this enough to give a wider view of society?

Would a form teacher have a different view of the purpose of education?

Is there any triangulation of findings using secondary sources? Should there be?

Do all the answers focus on the purpose of education? Do school staff represent a stratum of society that can be used to investigate 'today's world'? Is one stratum enough to answer this research question?

Activity: Evaluating the strengths and weaknesses of a piece of research

3 Complete the table by adding further strengths and weaknesses.

Strengths of Sadie's research	Weaknesses of Sadie's research
It is primary research, so Sadie has gone to experts to ask their views.	Sadie has not told us what questions were asked, but she has clearly focused on the purpose of education, as in the task.
All the answers show that Sadie focused on the purpose of education. She used a structured interview, however limited it was.	The question phrase 'in today's world' is looking for more than teachers' views. *Which groups of people could she have asked? What sort of a sample would have suited this?*
Sadie didn't just ask her subject teachers. *How did she make her research better by asking the head teacher and the form tutor?*	There is no secondary research to support or contradict these findings. There are journals about education that would carry perspectives on this topic. *Where and how could she have accessed these?*
She takes notes.	We don't know that she has told her interviewees about why she is asking these questions.
She has started off with an activity that is safe.	Teachers have a vested interest in the answers.

Activity: Analysing a piece of research

4 a Now use your notes to write an answer to the following practice question. You will need to go back to the complete version of Source 3 on page 99.

Practice questions

2 Study Source 3.

(a) Explain the strengths and weaknesses of the research outlined in Source 3. [8]

b Share your work with a partner, and ask them to check whether:

- you have explained both strengths and weaknesses
- the strengths and weaknesses are related to the aims of the research
- you have used the source to support your statements.

Apply

Final task

5 Work with a partner to plan and respond to the following practice question. You will need to use Source 7 on page 102.

Practice questions

2 Study Source 7.

(a) Explain the strengths and weaknesses of the research outlined in Source 7. [8]

6 Exchange answers with your partner and provide feedback.

Checklist for success

- ✔ Start by highlighting the focus of the research.
- ✔ Produce a table of the strengths and weaknesses and the evidence you have found.
- ✔ Explain both strengths and weaknesses.
- ✔ Use elements from the source to support your statements.

Reflective plenary

7 Discuss with a partner what you have learned about research methods.

Testing a claim

Skills focus

✓ Researching, analysing and evaluating information

Objective

- To design research to test a claim
- To justify the choices made in designing research

How do I test a claim that is made in an argument?

You have investigated a piece of research and found out its strengths and weaknesses. Now, it is time for you to plan a piece of research.

Starting point

1 In pairs, discuss your answer to this question, and the reasons for your answer.

If you wanted to find out how close we are to travel that puts ordinary people on the Moon, which source below would be more useful? How else could you investigate this issue?

Source A: A newspaper article about what very wealthy people are doing now

Source B: A journal from scientists about current research into space travel

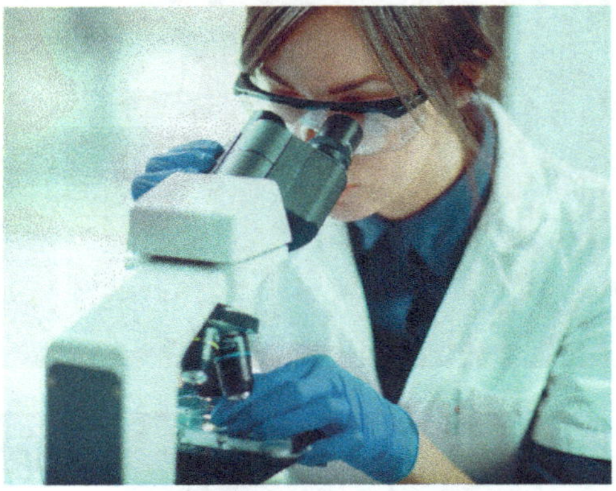

Explore

Testing a **claim** involves designing a piece of focused research. Look at the following practice question.

Practice questions

2 (b) 'Most teachers understand that teaching is about giving students the skills that they need for the future.'

Explain how this claim could be tested. You should consider the research methods and evidence that could be used. [8]

Note that the question gives you some guidance. You must consider:

- research methods you might use
- appropriate sources of evidence
- the types of evidence each method or source will give you
- the actions you would take and why you would take them
- how each part of your plan would help you to test the claim.

Key terms

claim: a statement or assertion made about an issue

Develop

Activity: Planning research

2 a Work with a partner to come up with some initial ideas of how you would test the claim in the practice question above.

b Now consider whether the following research methods and types of evidence could help you to test that claim.

Research method	The source of the evidence	Type of evidence	What would you learn from it? How reliable would your findings be?
Interviews	Teachers Parents Local businesspeople	Individual testimony/ **qualitative data**	You would need to keep data from each group separate – why?
Observing others (e.g. teachers)	Teachers and learners	Primary research data	Small scale, so would need to be triangulated.
Secondary research (from journals, books or websites)	Recent and international studies	Case studies Large scale studies Information from organisation interested in teaching	Interesting to compare to your primary research findings.
Questionnaires	Teachers Learners	Primary research data	Need to keep results separate. Interesting to compare.
Surveys	All teachers at school	Statistical evidence/ **quantitative data**	Gives a lot of information that can be used to check interview and observation findings.
Case studies	Teachers From journals	Qualitative data	This is the same as for secondary research.

Activity: Developing a research plan

3 With a partner, use the information in the table above to decide what methods you would use and how they could help you to reach an answer to the question. Two examples are given on the following page.

Key terms

qualitative data: views, ideas, experiences that add quality to a research report

observing others: this is a technique in which the researcher observes their subjects in a natural setting, without interfering; it can be a good introductory way of gathering information, but is open to the observer's bias, so needs triangulating

quantitative data: involving or relating to considerations of amount or size; giving figures that can be compared

Research method 1

A questionnaire to teachers in school

Reason: Primary research would give me information from experts that I could analyse to find out how much of their planning and teaching is focused on developing skills in learners to prepare them for future study or work. I could compare my findings to large-scale studies into the experience of teachers in schools.

Research method 2

A review of secondary research findings

Reason: In my primary research, I can only ask teachers in my school, in this country. This secondary research would give me information from other countries, and I could use it to triangulate my primary research findings. This would help me to answer the question because it would tell me if other countries had prioritised the skills that their learners need for the future.

Here is a sample answer to the question.

To test the claim that 'Most teachers understand that teaching is about giving students the skills that they need for the future', I would begin by asking teachers in my school what they think is the purpose of teaching. This sample population is best able to provide some data on the subject. To do this, I would first interview some teachers to get their personal views about what they think their role is mainly about. Because interviewing allows for investigative questioning, this would give me qualitative data to use in my research paper about whether teaching is mainly about giving us skills for the future.

However, because I might have chosen to interview people with unusual views, I would also write a questionnaire and survey all teachers in my school. This would give me quantitative data to use to triangulate my interview findings.

So far, I have limited my investigations to one school, and this may not be appropriate when the test is about 'Most teachers'. So, to correct this gap, I would carry out an online search to see if research has been carried out into what teachers see as their main purpose. I would look for recently carried out research, and research that brought the views of large numbers of teachers from different countries, as attitudes from different countries may differ about what teaching is for. This would confirm or challenge what my school offers as an answer about whether 'Most teachers understand teaching is about giving students the skills that they need for the future'.

Annotations:
- selects a method
- the evidence it provides
- linking back to the question
- issues with the first method and an explanation of the second method selected
- the evidence this would provide
- weaknesses so far, and the reason for another research method
- third research method
- the evidence this would provide
- brings it back to the question

Activity: Evaluating and improving an answer

4 Read the exemplar answer above. Look at it with a partner and analyse it to identify its strengths and weaknesses. Use the annotations provided to help you.

5 Now write your own answer to the practice question.
Remember to reference the question at each part of your answer:
I could do... because this would give me information about...
This would help me to answer the question because...

Apply

Final task

6 Now that you are clear about designing effective research, apply your learning to the second topic of Climate change, energy and resources. Plan and answer the following practice question, based on a statement taken from Source 7 on page 102.

Practice questions

2 **(b)** 'Most people want to buy fruit and vegetables grown locally.'
Explain how this claim could be tested. You should consider the research methods and evidence that could be used. [8]

Checklist for success

Remember to write about:

- ✔ the research methods and sources you might use
- ✔ the types of evidence these will provide
- ✔ the actions you would take and why you would take them
- ✔ how each part of your research plan would help you to test the claim.

Reflective plenary

7 Work with a partner. Exchange answers and give each other feedback.

8 Revisit your Starting point activity. Which research methods would you now use to find an answer?

Evaluating arguments

How do I compare the effectiveness of two arguments?

Starting point

1 In groups of four, take a one-minute challenge. One of you should argue *for* the statement 'frogs are more useful than cats', and one of you *against*. The other two listen. Have a vote on who was more convincing.

2 In pairs, create a spider diagram of features that made the arguments in activity 1 convincing. Think about the language used, evidence, reasoning and anything else you noticed.

Skills focus

✓ Researching, analysing and evaluating information

✓ Developing and justifying a line of reasoning

Objective

- To learn how to evaluate an argument
- To understand how to justify your judgement

Explore

In Global Perspectives, you may be asked to evaluate two **arguments** and decide which is more convincing.

You're going to begin by comparing the two arguments from Source 4 on page 100, using the following grid to guide your evaluation.

Which argument is more convincing?	Edie's argument (with quotations, where helpful)
Argument • What points are made? • Is the argument credible?	*She argues that Business Studies is based on real businesses through the use of case studies and that it is an academic subject that is relevant to future work.* *She argues that she can find out about the fashion industry that she wants to work in through her business studies lessons at school.* *Points:* • *fashion industry important nationally and internationally* • *teacher is good and has taught about different types of business and their functions, giving her an understanding and a sense of how she could fit in.* *Credible – within her experience, but she doesn't have external comparisons.* *Her statements reflect what others would expect from a Business Studies course.*

Key terms

argument: a series of statements containing reasons and evidence which support a claim about a global issue

Which argument is more convincing?	Edie's argument (with quotations, where helpful)
Reasoning • Is it logical and are her claims sensible and linked to the overall argument? • Is it well organised and structured? • Balance – does it acknowledge other viewpoints?	*Her argument is that Business Studies is an academic subject that teaches about a range of businesses and how they are organised.* *She is arguing that learning from case studies is a way of learning from businesses.* *The argument is sensible because students could not possibly visit all types of industries to learn from them. She evidences what she has learned clearly, showing the range of industries she has learned about and that they share many features in their organisation.* *The structure could be improved to state her argument clearly at the start.* *The argument is logical, going from industries to departments in the fashion industry.* *Her claims are sensible, showing how case studies from businesses help her to learn. She did not show us that the case studies are recent ones.* *Other viewpoints aren't looked into.*
Use of language • Is it clearly expressed and easy to follow? • What's the tone? Is it emotive, exaggerated, precise or measured?	*The tone is fairly neutral, but with an element of excitement and an emphatic tone: 'My Business Studies teacher in school is a really good teacher'; 'I have every confidence…'* *The expression is generally clear, though not precise: 'good teacher'; 'good exam results'.* *There is no exaggeration.*
Evidence • Is there a range of evidence? • How relevant is it? • Is there enough evidence? Are sample sizes big enough? • Where does the evidence come from? (source) Is it expert? • How recent is it?	*The range of evidence is limited and personal.* *What she describes is well explained and supported: 'analysed case studies from different types of businesses: from mining, to market stalls and from the creative industries.'* *The evidence is relevant, and recent.*
Bias or vested interest • Is there likely to be bias? • Can you identify any vested interest?	*No*
Consequences • What are the possible consequences of the ideas or actions presented in the argument?	*Families and young people listening might be persuaded that Business Studies is a relevant and appropriate course for their children.*
Values • How likely are other people to agree with this perspective/view?	*Adults might remember taking courses like this and would agree with the description of its usefulness.* *Teachers would agree that academic teaching of business is useful.*

Activity: Planning to evaluate two arguments

3 Read Edie's and Pablo's contributions to the radio show in Source 4.

a Work in pairs. Complete a grid like the one above for Pablo's argument, using the examples for Edie's argument to help you.

b Now colour-code the points in your grid to show whether they are strengths or weaknesses.

Develop

Now that you have completed a breakdown of the features of both arguments, read this practice question.

Practice questions

3 Which argument is more convincing, Edie's or Pablo's? Explain your answer fully.

Your answer should:

- consider both arguments
- evaluate their reasoning, evidence and use of language
- support your judgement with their words and ideas. [16 marks]

Activity: Analysing an answer

4 Read the extracts from a sample answer below and look at the annotations.

a Does it answer the question effectively?

b Do you agree with the judgement in the sample answer? Explain why.

Edie argues that Business Studies is an academic subject best learned through case studies. Pablo argues that the excitement of a virtual tour of a local business taught him more than he learned from books. I am going to analyse their arguments to find out whose argument is more convincing.

clearly states both the arguments as an introduction

Overall, Edie's argument is more convincing.

states an answer (in case you forget to do it at the end)

Edie shows that this is an academic subject by referencing exam results. She shows how the subject is taught by talking about case studies on mining and market stalls. This is relevant to the argument about how businesses are involved in teaching this subject. The detail she uses about the fashion industry such as the departments 'with different functions: Finance, Administration, Design and Development' makes her argument credible.

directly quotes from the source

discusses credibility of Edie's argument and uses some evidence from the source

The reasoning in Edie's argument is easy to follow: because the class works with case studies, they learn in detail about a range of businesses, from mining to the fashion industry. This is a sensible argument because it would not be possible to visit every kind of business to learn first-hand. By noting that students get good results, Edie provides evidence that this way of involving businesses is successful.

[...]

Pablo's argument is/isn't so credible because...

Overall, Edie's argument is more convincing because the reasoning is sound and her argument is based on a broader range of relevant evidence, while Pablo's argument is more personal and limited. Neither uses exaggeration, and while both might be biased in favour of their own experience, the possible outcomes for Edie's argument might be greater, encouraging more students to successfully study business.

makes clear what the focus of this paragraph is to be

reasoning showing business involvement through case studies to be effective

refers closely to the source

at this point in the answer, the student goes on to look at Edie's use of language, evidence, bias, consequences and any comments on values, following the structure of the grid

the student now goes on to consider Pablo's argument, following the structure of the grid

conclusion to draw together and show what the judgement is

Apply

You are now going to look at the sources on the topic of Climate change, and compare the arguments made by Qazi and Serena in Source 8 on page 103, using the process demonstrated above.

Practice questions

3 Study Source 8.

Which argument is more convincing, Serena's or Qazi's?

Your answer should:

- consider both arguments
- evaluate their reasoning, evidence and use of language
- support your judgement with their words and ideas. [16 marks]

Final task

5 Work in pairs to prepare and answer the practice question, using the evaluation grid to help you plan detailed points.

Reflective plenary

6 In pairs, add to your Starting point spider diagram any additional factors you need to use when analysing an argument.

Section 3 . Unit 7

Developing lines of reasoning to support a course of action 1

Skills focus

✓ Researching, analysing and evaluating information

✓ Developing and justifying a line of reasoning

Objective

- To evaluate evidence to decide on a recommendation
- To develop a clear line of reasoning to support your judgement

How can I make a recommendation based on reasoning?

Starting point

1 You're trying to decide what subjects to select for further study. What are the factors that influence you? Explain why to a partner, then share your ideas with the class.

Explore

In Units 3.1 to 3.6, you looked at four sources on the topic of Education for all. You're now going to focus on how to use these sources to argue for a particular course of action. The course of action will work as a solution to an issue raised through the sources: the purpose of education.

Look at the following practice question and the annotations around it.

Practice questions

4 A government wants to improve the economy by making changes to the education system. The following actions are being considered:

- Make free full-time secondary education compulsory.
- Make students study in the morning and do paid work in the afternoon.
- Make local businesses help to teach secondary age children.

Which **one** of these actions would you recommend to the government, and why?

In your answer, you should:

- state your recommendation
- give reasons and evidence to support your choice
- use the material in the sources and/or any of your own ideas
- consider different arguments and perspectives. [20 marks]

This is the focus of the question. Your argument should be about how far the course of action would improve the economy of the country.

You'll need to recommend one of these three options. While justifying your course of action, you'll also need to show how another option would not achieve the aim as well.

Select an option and state it.

Use a wide range of evidence and reasons to justify your choice.

Use clear reasoning and compare different perspectives or actions.

When you begin to plan your answer, you'll need to start by looking over the sources to gather evidence that might support the different options. This will help you to make a choice and develop your argument.

As before, the effectiveness of your argument and your reasoning are more important than which option you choose.

Activity: Gathering relevant arguments and evidence from the sources

2 With a partner, consider evidence from the sources to support a country aiming to improve its economy. Complete the table below. What is missing?

Ideas	Source	Arguments for	Arguments against	Evaluation of course of action and sources
Make free full-time secondary education compulsory				
	Source 1	Countries with the highest GDP have compulsory secondary education Says results are very important		Based on UN data, specifically about GDP, so reliable and relevant
	Source 2	Schools teach skills and problem-solving	Says he needs employees to be skilled for the workplace	Business, so expert about the economy. But also a parent, so divided in what he says
	Source 3			Experts in meeting national needs
	Source 4	Both were secondary school experiences		
Make students study in the morning and do paid work in the afternoon				
	Source 3			
	Source 4	Pablo found out about key business processes such as just in time ordering	Edie – Business Studies in school is better	Pablo made a single visit, so while relevant, limited value
Make local businesses help to teach secondary age children				
	Source 2	Skills of the workplace should be taught	No evidence – would they have time?	He is an expert in the restaurant industry
	Source 4			

Activity: Identifying which option is best supported

3 Now that you have competed your analysis, you should decide which of the options is best supported by the evidence in your table. State your chosen course of action.

Develop

Let us have a look at what a developed argument to support this course of action might look like, using the annotated analysis of an example answer to help.

Making free full-time secondary education compulsory would be the best way of improving the economy, according to the sources studied.

Evidence from the sources supports this conclusion. Source 1 includes a graph showing clearly that the countries with the highest GDP are those that have secondary education for all children. But, also, it shows that making only primary education compulsory achieves less, so it is not primary education alone that makes the difference. The information is based on credible sources (UN data) and the presentation in the form of a graph makes this analysis straightforward. Therefore, compulsory free full-time secondary education would undoubtedly improve the country's economy.

Other sources support this choice. While Source 2 suggests learners are not 'work ready' when they leave schools, Source 3 shows that the school curriculum is developed to make learners able to solve problems, something that is essential to businesses and the economy. Teachers and a restaurant owner are both experts, but evidence from a school can be better trusted to give a perspective on how the curriculum fits into national plans. Also, the restaurant owner wanted schools to teach skills that he valued within the curriculum, not for children to begin to work part time. He perhaps does not know how time-pressured teaching for the exams can be.

Pablo argues that real experience of business is more useful than school-based teaching. However, he hoped for a job from his visit which makes it difficult to trust his judgement. Also, he was given this experience by his secondary school so it actually supports free secondary education as the action. All businesses could not supply schools with this sort of solution, and, anyway, not all schools are in industrial areas. Some students would want work from other sectors of the economy.

Annotations:

- opens by clearly stating which option
- clear, convincing line of reasoning; each paragraph focuses on a point and supports it with evidence and evaluation
- uses all sources; includes a wide range of evidence
- consistently relevant to the issue in the question
- well-structured and explicit comparison of perspectives
- judgements clearly related to the issue and clearly explained, consistent with the argument
- judgements are clearly related to the issue and clearly explained, consistent with the argument
- final judgement is consistent with the arguments made

In terms of practicality and impact, this action is also more effective. Asking students to get paid work would not benefit all of them equally, as not all employers will provide them with a broad enough training or have time to support students. There is also the practical issue of having to manage any relationship with employers and businesses.

The evidence overwhelmingly supports the option to make all students attend secondary school full time. It may be costly for the government, but the investment pays off with clear economic benefits as is shown so clearly in the UN data in Source 1!

final judgement is consistent with the arguments made

Activity: Analysing a sample answer

4 Read the answer above.

  a Highlight or identify where each source is referred to.

  b What does the answer do well?

  c How could the answer be improved?

Apply

Final task

5 Now write your own answer that selects one of the three options to improve the economy.

Checklist for success

- ✔ Use and develop ideas found in the sources but go beyond simply repeating them.
- ✔ Use clear reasoning, supported by evidence from the sources to support the course of action.
- ✔ Consider a range of arguments and perspectives.
- ✔ Refer back to the question.
- ✔ Make sure your arguments are appropriate and convincingly support the option you have chosen.
- ✔ Consider practical aspects of the solution: how long it would take to put in place, how easy this would be, any barriers, the cost, as well as the impact.

Reflective plenary

6 Share your answers in pairs. Give each other feedback using the checklist above.

Developing lines of reasoning to support a course of action 2

Skills focus
✓ Researching, analysing and evaluating information
✓ Developing and justifying a line of reasoning

Objective
- To learn how to evaluate evidence to decide on the recommended course of action
- To understand how to develop a clear line of reasoning to support your judgement

How can I make a recommendation based on reasoning?

In this unit, you will be applying the skills and process you developed in Unit 3.7 to recommend a course of action based on reasoning. You will be working with the sources on the topic of Climate change, energy and resources, and focusing on the issue of how best to reduce carbon emissions.

Starting point

1 First step. Work with a partner to identify the key words in this practice question.

Practice questions

4 A scientific policy group is considering how to advise its government on how best to reduce carbon emissions.

The following actions are being considered:

- Send a letter to every family explaining how they can help.
- Give grants to local industries to invest in new technology.
- Ask people to turn down their air conditioning and use less electricity.

Which **one** of these suggestions would you recommend to the government, and why?

In your answer, you should:

- state your recommendation
- give reasons to support your recommendation
- use the material in the sources and/or any of your own ideas
- consider different arguments and perspectives. [20 marks]

Explore

You are now going to work through the same process of evidence gathering and planning that you used in Unit 3.7.

Activity: Planning stage: analysing the different options

2 a Work in pairs to complete the planning grid below.

b Make notes on the impact of the action and on practical considerations such as potential cost, how difficult it will be to implement, any barriers to this, how long it will take to make a difference.

Planning				
Ideas	Relevant sources	Arguments for	Arguments against	Evaluation of the source/ the course of action
Option 1: Send a letter to every family explaining how they can help	General comments			Sending letter is cheap, personal and could be effective – even small changes help. Good to link to the UN campaign? Might need to back up letter with advertising/media campaign for more impact.
	Source 5	Two thirds of global emissions come from private households (UN)		UN responsible body giving guidance to countries – reliable guidance
	Source 6			
	Source 7			
	Source 8			
Option 2: Give grants to local industries to invest in new technology	General comments			Grants – development time is long, it takes longer to see effects. Will it be too costly?
	Source 5		Two-thirds of carbon emissions are linked to domestic use – so if we have just one action, is this the right focus?	
	Source 6	Technology already exists, and source shows it works		Is an example. What can other industries, e.g. air travel, do? Advice is to learn from other countries. Not all countries have biomass to burn.
	Source 7			
	Source 8			
Option 3: Ask people to turn down their air conditioning and use less electricity	Source 5	Reduce use of electricity, coal or gas		Is part of advice to families in option 1. Not all homes have air conditioning.

Apply

Final task

3 Plan and write your answer, using your thoughts on what makes a strong answer from 3.7 and the checklist on the right.

Reflective plenary

4 Create a class gallery of your answers. Read the work of others in your class. Return to your own work and note one thing that you would want to improve or add.

Checklist for success

- ✔ Use and develop ideas found in the sources but go beyond simply repeating them.
- ✔ Use clear reasoning, supported by evidence from the sources to support the course of action.
- ✔ Consider a range of arguments and perspectives.
- ✔ Refer back to the question regularly.
- ✔ Make sure your arguments are appropriate and convincingly support the option you have chosen.

Check your progress

▲ I can read a source with understanding.

I can locate information in a source.

I can identify a perspective or someone's ideas from a source.

I can give an opinion on an issue from a source.

I can identify a strength and a weakness in a piece of research.

I can plan to use at least one research method appropriate to test a claim.

I can explain the choices I made in designing research.

I can identify a strength and a weakness in an argument.

I can identify reasons why one argument is more convincing than another.

I can select a course of action to address an issue and explain my choice.

▲▲ I can describe what a source is about.

I can accurately locate information in a source and explain it with some understanding.

I can identify a perspective and some of the elements that make up the perspective.

I can give my opinion on an issue with some justifications.

I can explain strengths and weaknesses in a piece of research.

I can plan to use a range of research methods appropriate to test a claim.

I can justify the choices I made in designing research.

I can explain and analyse strengths and weaknesses in an argument, looking at some aspects of the argument such as reasoning and evidence, language, bias or consequences.

I can explain reasons why one argument is more convincing than another.

I can develop a line of reasoning to explain a chosen course of action.

▲▲▲ I can explain fully the meaning of a source.

I can clearly explain the meaning of information I have identified.

I can identify a perspective and analyse a wide range of elements that make up the perspective.

I can give my opinion on an issue with a range of relevant and convincing justifications.

I can give a reasoned evaluation of the strengths and weaknesses in a piece of research, including a wide range of points precisely and in detail.

I can plan to use a wide range of research methods and evidence types appropriate to test a claim.

I can effectively justify with reasons the choices I made in designing research.

I can effectively analyse the strengths and weaknesses in an argument, looking at a range of aspects of the argument such as reasoning and evidence, language, bias and consequences.

I can effectively justify my evaluation of the argument.

I can write convincingly, developing a line of reasoning to support a chosen course of action.

Next steps

- If you are interested in the issue of education or climate change, identify aspects that you would like to know more about. Who could you ask or where could you look to find out about the local or national situation? How would you record your findings?

Section 4: Writing an individual report

4

This section explores the process of carrying out and writing a research project. The examples in this section focus on the issue of conservation. You will be asked to decide on your own issue as a group and develop your own research project in parallel to the examples. You should choose a global issue to focus on that has an impact in your community. As part of your investigation, you will need to consider a range of different perspectives: global, national and local. Working together with the members of your team, you will need to conduct your own research to locate sources containing these perspectives.

The example investigation focuses on the syllabus topic 'Environment, pollution and conservation' and also touches on 'Water, food and agriculture'. The examples of work in this investigation have been written by our authors.

Your final task will be to write substantial sections of an essay in response to the question that you formulate with your group.

You will be developing the following skills:

Research and analysis

4.1 Exploring a topic, choosing an issue and formulating a research question

4.2 Identifying, analysing and engaging with perspectives

4.3 Analysing the issue and its causes and consequences

4.4 Researching different courses of action to help solve the issue

Essay writing

4.5 Making a plan for your essay

4.6 Writing an introduction

4.7 Discussing causes and consequences

4.8 Selecting perspectives and describing them in your essay

4.9 Writing about evaluating sources

4.10 Making judgements about perspectives

4.11 Reflecting on your developing personal perspective

4.12 Making a case for a course of action

4.13 Writing a conclusion

4.14 Writing a bibliography for your report.

Group work and peer-assessment activities are included throughout this chapter. When you tackle your real Individual Report, you will need to work independently, and you will have to manage your own time to complete the report successfully. We hope the chapter will provide a useful reference point when you come to do this, and that you will be able to look back at the stages and activities outlined to help you manage the process.

Exploring a topic, choosing an issue and formulating a research question

Skills focus
✓ Researching, analysing and evaluating information

Objective
- To formulate an appropriate research question

How can I make sure that I have a good question to research?

In this unit, you are going to be preparing to research and write your Individual Report. The following units take you through the process of identifying a global issue, carrying out research, then planning and writing your report. You will be able to develop your own report, working with an issue that you choose, in parallel with the process demonstrated here.

Starting point

1 Look at the list of syllabus topics.

Arts in society
Development, trade and aid
Environment, pollution and conservation
Law and criminality
Poverty and inequality
Water, food and agriculture
Change in culture and communities
Digital world
Social identity and inclusion
Media and communication
Sport and recreation
Values and beliefs
Climate change, energy and resources
Education for all
Globalisation
Migration and urbanisation
Technology, industry and innovation
Conflict and peace
Employment
Health and wellbeing
Political power and action
Transport, travel and tourism

When you are asked to complete an individual research report, you will need to find an issue that interests you and frame a research question to investigate. Which three topics interest you most? What do you know already? What would you be interested in finding out? Make some notes, then compare your ideas with a partner.

Explore

In this unit, you will learn how to formulate an appropriate research question for a Global Perspectives Essay. This is because you will want to explore an issue that gives enough scope to explore contrasting perspectives – but be manageable in the time you have available.

Sitaram has selected the topic Environment, pollution and conservation to focus on. This is because it is a global issue. It has impacts in his locality and he would like to find out more about the global situation. He knows that this issue is one that causes both hardship and disagreement. He identified some issues in this topic that he knows about. Two of them are listed below. He has devised globally focused questions that he is interested in exploring.

Issues that I know something about	What I would be interested in exploring globally
Air pollution is an issue in local cities – chemicals from burning plastic. Particles from traffic.	What policies have been successful in reducing air pollution in other cities globally?
Biodiversity loss. We have national parks in our state. Endangered species (e.g. tiger) are recovering. This has taken a lot of effort.	Have our national parks done a good job? Could other countries learn from our approach?

Activity: Exploring a topic

2 a Work with a partner. Select a topic to explore.
  b What issues do you know about, locally or nationally, that arise from this topic? Make a list.
  c What questions would you be interested in exploring on these issues? Think globally.

Develop

Sitaram has selected the issue of **biodiversity** loss. He has checked if this issue has potential. He asked himself these questions:

- Is it a global issue?
- Is it contentious? (It is important to choose an issue that divides opinion.)
- Does it have a range of impacts in today's world that I can explore?

Here is Sitaram's mind map that he created to choose an issue.

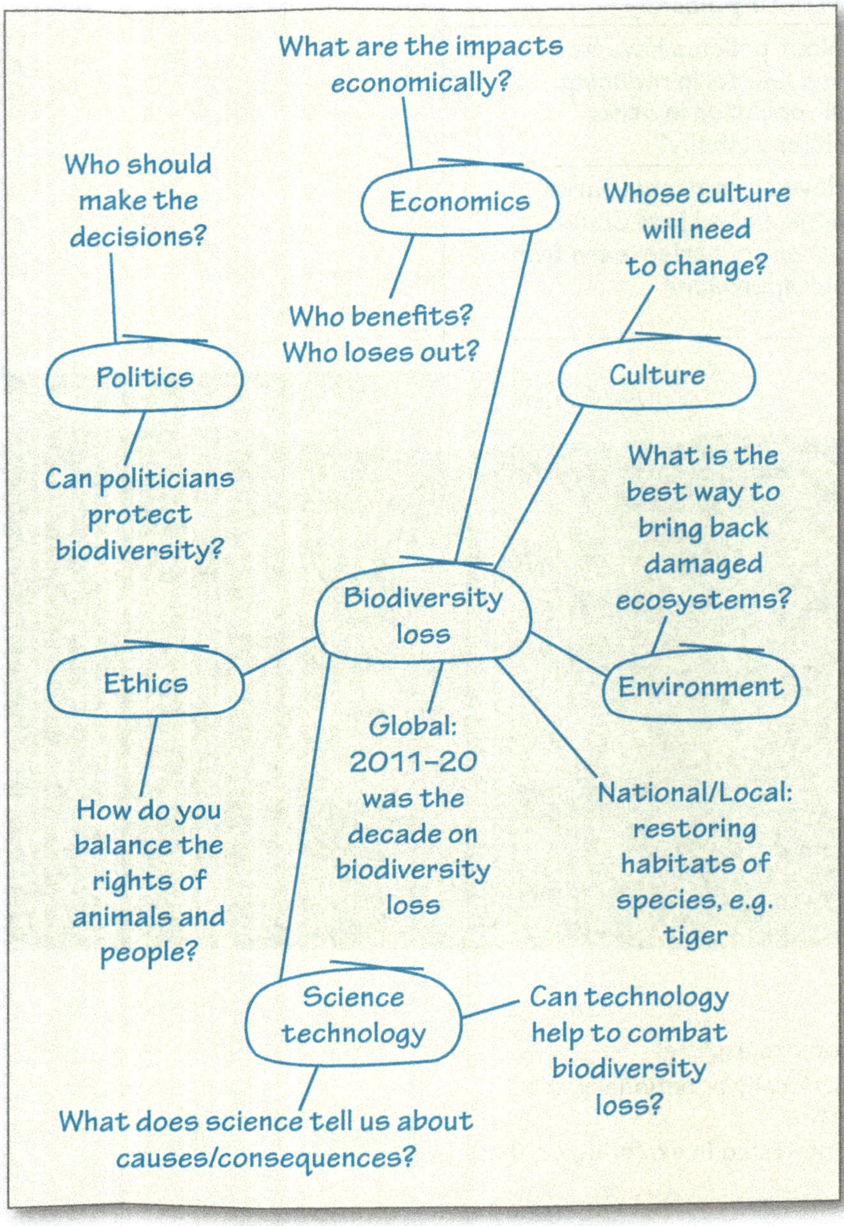

Vocabulary

biodiversity: the variety of plant and animal life in the world

Key terms

ethics: moral values; the rules and principles that should govern human conduct

economics: the study of the way in which money, industry and trade are organised

politics: actions or activities concerned with achieving and using power in a country or society

culture: the beliefs, habits and way of life of a people or a society

Activity: Choosing a potential issue

3 a Work with a partner. Select some issues that you identified in activity 2. Check if these issues have potential. For each one, ask yourselves:

- Is it a local issue? Is it a global issue?
- Is it something that is contentious and will spark debate?
- Does it have a modern-day impact?
- Does it have a range of aspects that you could explore?

b Capture the main points of your discussion in mind maps.

c Now share your ideas with your teacher.

Study skills

When you work on your own issue for your Individual Report, you will need to work independently of others.

Activity: Researching an issue

4 Conduct some further research on the issue you have identified with your partner. Develop your mind map by:

- researching different perspectives in the media
- listening to relevant podcasts
- talking to people you know and asking for their views.

Study skills

When you research, don't forget to complete a log entry for your sources, using the format from Unit 2.4.1. Remember to include details about the perspective, any questions it raises, who produced the source and so on.

Apply

Sitaram has refined one of his questions.

'What is the best way to bring back damaged ecosystems?'

He changed it to:

'Should we use **rewilding** to restore damaged ecosystems?'

- A single global issue ✓ Should we use rewilding?
- National/Local perspectives ✓ Should we use rewilding here?
- Contrasting perspectives ✓ We should vs we should not.

Vocabulary

rewilding: the practice of returning areas of land to a wild state, including the reintroduction of animal species that are no longer naturally found there

Final task

5 Work with a partner. Refine some of your questions. Make sure that your questions allow you to explore:
- a single global issue
- national/local perspectives
- contrasting perspectives.

6 Share your refined questions with a small group. Discuss the issues and the different perspectives on these issues. Look at each other's mind maps. What issue are you going to choose to develop over the course of this unit? Ask yourselves:
- Is it a global issue?
- Does it have impacts?
- Does it cause difficulty/hardship/conflicts/disagreement?
- Can we explore different perspectives on this issue?

7 Now share your group's ideas with your teacher.

Reflective plenary

8 How would you complete the following sentence?

When I do my individual report, I will need to select an issue for myself. I will need to make sure that…

Identifying, analysing and engaging with perspectives

Skills focus
✓ Researching, analysing and evaluating information
✓ Developing and justifying a line of reasoning

Objective
- To form a reasoned response to a perspective

How should I engage with a perspective?

Starting point

1 Think about an issue that is currently in the news. Think of a perspective that someone has expressed on the issue. To what extent do you agree with that perspective? Make some brief notes, then explain your answer to a partner.

Explore

In this unit, you will learn how to identify, analyse and engage with perspectives.

When you do research for an individual report, it is important to identify different perspectives on your issue. You will need to set out a *discussion* in your essay, and it is much easier to set out a discussion on an issue that divides opinion – therefore, you need to find those opinions, not just information about the issue. A common misconception is to find out facts about a topic and think that this is all that is required.

In addition, you will need to engage with different perspectives for yourself. Another common misconception is that you can just set out other people's ideas. Instead, you need to reach your own judgements about the issue. This unit will take you through the process.

Sitaram has conducted some initial research on his issue. Below, he has set out his understanding of different perspectives. He has also engaged with these perspectives and made a judgement. He can develop these ideas when he writes his report. Different sections of his argument have been highlighted with different colours.

Topic: Environment, pollution and conservation

Issue: Biodiversity loss

Question: Should we use rewilding to restore damaged ecosystems?

Biodiversity loss caused by human activity is severe. Urgent action is needed to restore damaged ecosystems. Some in the scientific community believe that 'rewilding' is an idea whose time has come. Rewilding projects reintroduce species to areas they used to live in. Allowing magnificent creatures to roam in their former habitats seems like an attractive option – but others argue that there are significant risks.

There is no doubt that human activity has been a major cause of biodiversity loss. Human hunting has always had an impact on ecosystems. Industrial pollution and intensive agriculture have massively increased the rate of species loss. In India, Chandra and Chandra (2015) have shown how the situation was worsened because the **colonial** administration permitted **indiscriminate** hunting. Tragically, many species, such as cheetahs, are now extinct locally. Tigers, rhinos and elephants remain critically endangered.

Rewilding projects have reintroduced large animals to their former homes. Supporters of this idea like Jepson argue that reintroducing creatures can restore balance to damaged ecosystems. Conservationists like the idea of allowing nature the time and space to heal itself. The process of bringing back species that used to live in an area repairs human damage. They even say that the healthy ecosystems created could combat climate change.

On the other hand, it is argued that rewilding projects are reckless. They can create significant problems. Nogués-Bravo and his colleagues (2016, cited in *Science Daily*) argue that introducing large new creatures to an existing ecosystem is expensive and the results can be unpredictable. Some rewilding success stories have received a lot of publicity. In many cases, positive results are hard to prove. There are also cases where rewilding projects have caused actual damage to ecosystems.

There is clearly an urgent need to increase biodiversity. Rewilding projects seem to be too much of a gamble. Nogués-Bravo and his colleagues argue that strategies like tackling **invasive species** and protecting forests are cheaper and have proven to be more effective. We need to be sure that we can control the risks. Until we have certainty, it seems sensible to promote biodiversity by using proven methods.

Sitaram has provided a clear reference to the authors' study here. Full details will be given in his bibliography (see Unit 4.14).

Here, Sitaram shows he did not use Nogués-Bravo's source directly. He has paraphrased from the *Science Daily* article summary.

Vocabulary

colonial: colonialism is the practice by which one country directly controls other countries and uses their resources to increase its own power and wealth

Vocabulary

indiscriminate: without careful thought or choice

invasive species: an animal or plant that is not native to an ecosystem, that has been introduced by humans and can cause damage

Activity: Defining the issue

2 a What topic is Sitaram researching?
  b What is his issue?
  c What question is he focusing on?

Activity: Developing an overview of the perspectives

3 Work with a partner to match the highlighting colour to the section. The first one has been done for you. Sections:

- Causes
- Consequences
- Actions
- Perspectives in favour
- Perspectives against
- Personal judgement on the perspectives.

Activity: Identifying your own perspectives

4 Work with a small group.
  a Select a global topic to discuss from the syllabus list.
  b Identify an issue.
  c Frame a question around this issue. (Tip: make sure the question would lead to a clear for/against discussion.)
  d What contrasting perspectives do you think there will be on this issue?
  e Now share your group's ideas with your teacher.

Study skills

When you work on your own issue for your Individual Report, you will need to work independently of others.

Develop

When someone gives a viewpoint on an issue, they give a judgement – for example, 'It is right.' When someone gives a *perspective*, they offer evidence and reasoning in support of their judgement.

We will look at evidence in more detail later in the unit. For now, we will concentrate on reasoning.

Sitaram has analysed the perspective in favour of rewilding.

Perspective	Judgement	Reasoning
For rewilding	Rewilding projects should be supported because they restore balance.	Humans have caused damage. Species that used to thrive in an ecosystem have been wiped out. It is right to put them back.

Activity: Analysing a perspective

5 Work with a partner to analyse the perspective against rewilding.

Perspective	Judgement	Reasoning
Against rewilding		

Activity: Analysing our own perspectives

6 Work with a small group. Discuss the contrasting perspectives that you identified on your chosen issue in activity 4. What judgements would each side make? What reasoning would they offer in support of that judgement?

Perspective	Judgement	Reasoning
For ___________		
Against ___________		

Apply

Sitaram has set out his judgement in his final paragraph. This is based on the research he has conducted so far. His question is: *Should we use rewilding to restore damaged ecosystems?*

Final task

7 Discuss with a partner:

- **a** Which side of the argument (for or against) does Sitaram support?
- **b** What reason does he give for making this judgement?

8 Work individually. What is your judgement about the issue you discussed in activity 6? Use the research you carried out in Unit 4.1, activity 4, along with your prior understanding and the discussions that you had with your group.

- **a** Which side of the argument (for or against) do you support?
- **b** What reason(s) would you give for making this judgement?

9 Work in a small group. What judgements do members of the group make about the issue you have been discussing?

- **a** Which side of the argument (for or against) do they support?
- **b** What reasons do they give for making their judgements?
- **c** How does their reasoning affect your own judgement? Explain your answer.
- **d** Now share your group's ideas with your teacher.

Reflective plenary

10 Complete these sentences.

When I write my Individual Report, I will not just find out facts about a topic. I will research perspectives. This is important because…

When I write my Individual Report, I will not just set out perspectives, I will engage with them. This is important because…

Analysing the issue and its causes and consequences

Skills focus

✓ Developing and justifying a line of reasoning

Objective

- To analyse the causes and consequences of your global issue

How do I analyse the causes and consequences of my chosen issue?

Starting point

1 Think of a time when you were late for something. What caused you to be late? What were the consequences?

Explore

In this unit, you will learn how to identify the causes and consequences of your global issue. You are much more likely to frame an appropriate course of action or suggest an effective solution if you understand the causes and consequences of your issue.

Sitaram has found two sources:

Source 1 Rewilding: a climate change solution by Dr Paul Jepson

During the Pleistocene period (roughly 2.5 million to 12,000 years ago), extensive areas of the Arctic were covered with grassland – this was naturally grazed by herds of bison, horses, woolly rhinoceros and mammoths. But when humans moved into these so-called 'mammoth steppe' areas, unsustainable levels of hunting meant populations of these large herbivores collapsed, and some became extinct. As a result, the grassland gave way to boggy, peat-forming vegetation.

Vocabulary

khedah: an enclosure into which wild elephants are driven to be captured

Source 2 Chandra & Chandra, from *Reparation for destruction of wildlife: That'll be 15bn Pounds, your Highness*

The ecological impoverishment of India has been chronicled graphically in the personal diaries, memoirs and photos of British officers who ruled India. The British hunted tigers, cheetahs and leopards with high-velocity rifles, speared bears and conducted **khedah**-catching of elephants for ivory. They invented the logic that hunting was good for the development of 'character', and that it trained young men to be good soldiers.

Between 1875 and 1925, at least 50,000 tigers were slain.

Cheetahs, which once roamed freely, are extinct today. Tigers, rhinos and elephants remain endangered species. Since 1971, when Project Tiger was launched, it has taken scarce resources and 45 years of rigorous effort at various levels to raise tiger numbers by about 300.

Activity: Identifying causes and consequences

2 Analyse each source individually, then compare your findings in pairs. You may also use your own prior knowledge.

Question	Source 1	Source 2
a What damage has been caused?		
b Where did this take place?		
c Who caused the damage?		
d Why?		
e What long-term consequences have there been?		

The British Prince of Wales (later King George V) on an official visit to India in 1906

Develop

Activity: Analysing causes and consequences

3 Work with a small group. Compare your answers to activity 2, then discuss these questions.

a What causes and consequences can be found in both sources?

b What differences do you notice?

Apply

Sitaram is talking about his research.

> In the Arctic, the ecosystem changed 12,000 years ago. That must have an impact on rewilding projects. Habitats take a long time to change. In India, the species loss was more recent. Maybe there's more chance of success. On the other hand, the loss of species was rapid. 45 years of hard work has had limited results. Even if you stopped all hunting globally, that would not guarantee success in the short term. I'm thinking that there is not a 'one size fits all' solution here.

Activity: What are the implications?

4 Work individually to answer these questions, then compare your thoughts with a partner.

a What comparison does Sitaram make?

b What implications has he drawn for his course of action?

Final task

5 Work individually, then compare your thoughts with a small group, to answer the following questions about your own issue. You may refer back to the research you did for Unit 4.1.

a What causes of your issue can you identify?

b What are the consequences?

c What barriers will need to be overcome?

6 Now share your group's ideas with your teacher.

Study skills

When you work on your own issue for your Individual Report, you will need to work independently of others.

Reflective plenary

7 Complete these sentences.

When I study a global issue for my Individual Report, I will need to study the causes and consequences of my global issue.

It is important to understand causes because…

It is important to understand consequences because…

Researching different courses of action to help solve the issue

Skills focus

✓ Researching, analysing and evaluating information

Objective

- To identify appropriate courses of action
- To explain how they can be implemented
- To explain how they will solve the issue

How should I explain my course of action?

Starting point

1 Think about an everyday issue, such as forgetting equipment for a lesson. What caused this issue? What were the consequences? What steps did you take to resolve the issue? How effective was your strategy?

Explore

In this unit, you will learn how to identify an appropriate course of action in response to the issue you have chosen. An effective course of action will deal with the causes – or **mitigate** the consequences, or both!

Vocabulary

mitigate: reduce the impact of

Sitaram searched for 'podcast rewilding' and found this discussion, which includes suggested courses of action.

Presenter:	So, what's the answer?
Speaker 1:	Well, we can stop farming altogether. Farming causes ecosystem damage.
Presenter:	Seriously, who's saying that?
Speaker 1:	Well, UK based environmentalist George Monbiot for one.
Presenter:	But people have still got to eat – right?
Speaker 1:	Right, but you can eat food that's grown in labs. Lab grown protein can replace meat, fish, eggs. Almost everything that comes out of a farm now can come out of a factory in the future. You hand all of that farmland back to nature. All that endangered plant and animal life gets a chance to recover.
Speaker 2:	Look, many contest this whole idea of lab food.
Presenter:	Farmers presumably.
Speaker 2:	Not just farmers. Take Vandana Shiva for one – a distinguished Indian scholar. She argues that high tech food is fake food. We must keep farming.
Presenter:	But haven't we just found out that it's agriculture that's basically causing the ecosystem damage?
Speaker 2:	Not all farming. Farming driven by profit is the problem. Intensive farming that is heavy on chemical use. Intensive farming wastes energy and causes long-term damage. The idea of lab food comes from the same wrong thinking.
Speaker 1:	But we need the space to rewild.
Speaker 2:	Shiva says you can rewild farming. What is agriculture? 'Care for the earth' is her answer. She would argue that 'Real farming is farming with nature, in nature's ways, which are the laws of ecology'. So according to her, you can grow 'healthy food by conserving biodiversity through abundant **pollinators** and thriving soil **organic** matter'.

Sitaram summarised the second speaker's perspective below.

Solution/Course of action	How it will be implemented	How it will address the issue
Rewild farming	Change farming methods. Farm, with nature. Organic soil.	'Real' farming protects biodiversity. Plants get pollinated. Insects recover.

Activity: Summarising a perspective

2 Work with a partner. Summarise the first speaker's perspective using a table like the one above.

Develop

Which of the two speakers do you find most persuasive?

Activity: Who convinces me?

3 Work with a partner. Use the discussion above and your own prior understanding to answer these questions.

a Which speaker do you think has proposed the more effective solution?

b Why do you think this?

Activity: Who convinces us?

4 Discuss your answers to activity 3 in a small group.

Apply

Now focus on the global issue you have been researching with your group.

Final task

5 a Try searching online for 'solutions' or 'podcast' or 'actions to deal with' and then your issue to see if you find any helpful sources.

b Discuss these questions in a small group.

- What solutions can you come up with for your global issue?
- How could they be implemented?
- How would they resolve the issue?
- Which one do you find most convincing?
- Why is this?

c Now share your group's ideas with your teacher.

Vocabulary

pollinators: things that pollinate plants, especially some types of insects, e.g. bees

organic: farming and gardening using only natural animal and plant products rather than using chemicals

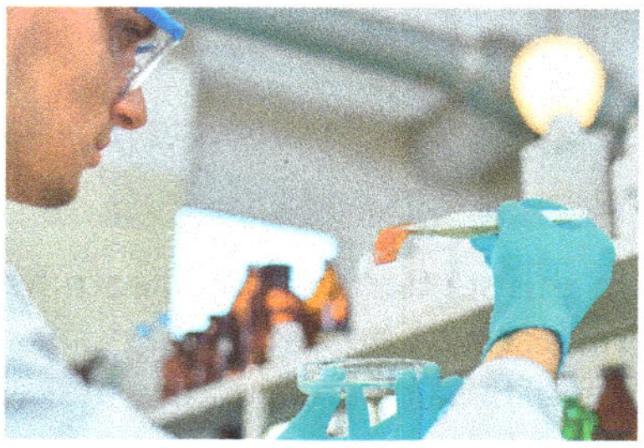

Study skills

When you work on your own issue for your Individual Report, you will need to work independently of others.

Reflective plenary

6 How would you finish this sentence?

When I am researching courses of action for my own Individual Report, I will need to make sure that I look for…

Making a plan for your essay

Skills focus
- ✓ Researching, analysing and evaluating information
- ✓ Developing and justifying a line of reasoning
- ✓ Communicating information and reasoning

Objective
- To understand how to plan a successful research report

How should I plan my report writing?

Starting point

1 Think about how you have planned substantial pieces of work in other subjects. What strategies have you found to be successful?

Explore

In this section, you will learn how to put together a plan for your report writing. Effective plans make it easier to write well-structured reports. A clear structure makes your argument easy to follow and, therefore, more convincing.

Sitaram is discussing his project with his teacher, Ms Nambiar, in a lesson on report writing skills.

Ms Nambiar:	Tell me about your global issue.
Sitaram:	My global issue is biodiversity loss, and I will be asking if we should use rewilding to solve the issue.
Ms Nambiar:	What are the causes of this issue?
Sitaram:	Intensive farming has taken up land. You've got hunting, climate change, pollution and invasive species.
Ms Nambiar:	And what are the consequences?
Sitaram:	It could not be more serious. The whole planet depends on healthy ecosystems.
Ms Nambiar:	What perspectives will you explore?
Sitaram:	Perspectives for and against rewilding as a global solution.
Ms Nambiar:	Is there a national or local dimension to this issue?
Sitaram:	Ecosystem damage was severe in the colonial period. Locally, we have important wildlife sanctuaries. I will talk about the consequences of these, like farmers who have been resettled.
Ms Nambiar:	Tell me about your sources. Have you evaluated them?
Sitaram:	I have tried to find the most credible supporter of each perspective that I can find. Shiva is a leading advocate of sustainable farming. Jepson for rewilding.
Ms Nambiar:	What course of action will you be supporting and why?
Sitaram:	We can do a lot by changing the way we farm. Better farming will lead to better biodiversity. You also have to look at who owns the land.
Ms Nambiar:	Tell me about your personal perspective. What was it at the start of your research and how did it develop?
Sitaram:	At first, I just thought rewilding was a good idea. Then I found out more about the downsides – it is unpredictable. Then I came round more to the sustainable farming perspective.
Ms Nambiar:	So what is your overall conclusion?
Sitaram:	Ok, my question is 'Should we use rewilding to restore damaged ecosystems?' Essentially the answer is 'yes' – but huge care is needed. We can't just throw farmers off their land and bring in the carnivores.

Sitaram has started his report plan.

Issue: Biodiversity has been hit. Should we rewild?

Causes: Species loss caused by human activity.

Consequences: Different perspectives – positive or negative consequences.

Actions: Rewilding and/or sustainable farming discussion.

Introduction		
Paragraph 2		
Paragraph 3	The 'for' and 'against' rewilding perspectives: • pro main source: Jepson (2020) • benefits for the Arctic and restoring ecosystems • downside – it is unpredictable	350 words
Paragraph 4		
Paragraph 5		
Conclusion		
	Total	2000 words

Activity: Developing a plan

2 Work with a partner. How should Sitaram complete this plan? Aim to include all of the main points from the discussion.

Develop

Activity: Comparing plans

3 Explain your version of Sitaram's plan to your group. Listen to theirs. Which one was the easiest to follow? Explain why.

Apply

Activity: Discussing our issue

4 Role-play the questions that Sitaram was asked by Ms Nambiar for your own issue. How would you answer them?

Final task

5 a How would you structure your report? Work as a group to complete a plan using a grid like the one in activity 2.

Issue:

Causes:

Consequences:

Actions:

b Now share your group's ideas with your teacher.

Study skills

Your teacher can help direct you in your research and organisational *skills*. Your teacher can't undertake any research for you or suggest amendments to your Individual Report.

Study skills

When you work on your own issue for your Individual Report, you will need to work independently of others.

Reflective plenary

6 Think about when you will write your Individual Report. How would you finish this sentence?

My plan will need to include... This is because...

Writing an introduction

What should I put in my introduction?

Skills focus
- ✓ Researching, analysing and evaluating information
- ✓ Communicating information and reasoning

Objective
- To learn how to write an introduction to your report

Starting point

1 What advice have you been given in other subjects about what goes in an introduction? Will the advice be relevant here? Make brief notes, then compare your ideas in pairs.

Explore

In this unit, you will learn how to write a good introduction for your research report. An effective introduction sets up your report and is crucial to its **cohesion**.

Ms Nambiar has given Sitaram a few bullet points to help him write his introduction:

Key terms

cohesion: something that is cohesive consists of parts that fit together well and form a united whole

Checklist for success
- Make sure I know what your issue is.
- Make sure I understand why your issue is a global one.
- Make sure I know why your issue is important. Tell me why I should care.
- Tell me what perspectives you will discuss.
- Tell me why people disagree.
- Keep it short – 250 words max.
- Give me an overview of the discussion that will follow.
- Use plain and simple language.

Here is Sitaram's introduction.

Should we use rewilding to restore damaged ecosystems?

A healthy planet Earth depends on healthy ecosystems. Ecosystems are best understood as the way organisms interact with each other. 'Around 1 million animal and plant species are threatened with extinction' according to the Global Assessment Report on Biodiversity and Ecosystem Service (UN 2019). Nature is 'under stress'. The planet is losing species at an ever-increasing rate. I will examine the causes of biodiversity loss. These causes include clearing forests to make way for intensive farming. I will also consider the serious consequences for humans. If this issue is not resolved, the consequences could include food insecurity globally and more pandemics. Governments will need to make decisions. What policies can help? 'Rewilding' is one possibility. Rewilding is defined as the 'practice of returning areas of land to a wild state, including the reintroduction of animal species that are no longer naturally found there' (*Collins Dictionary*). I will examine ecosystem loss nationally and locally. Many Indian species are endangered. I will ask if rewilding is appropriate here. Supporters make big claims. They argue that rewilding is a way of giving nature a helping hand so the planet can heal itself. They say that it plays a major role in stopping climate change. Critics say that it is an unproven strategy. They claim that rewilding projects have unpredictable consequences. Some say the strategy is based on wrong-thinking about people being separate from nature. I will discuss both these global perspectives, and this discussion will guide my course of action and overall conclusion.

Activity: Giving feedback about an introduction

2 Work with a partner. Discuss how well Sitaram met Ms Nambiar's criteria.

Develop

Activity: Looking at language

3 Some phrases from Sitaram's introduction above have been highlighted. This is because they could be useful for you to use in an introduction about *any* issue. Are there any others? In pairs, make a list.

Apply

Final task

4 Work with a partner. Draft an introduction to a report about the issue you have been discussing.

5 Swap your introduction with another pair. Give them feedback, using Ms Nambiar's points. What went well and what could they improve?

6 Now share your introduction with your teacher.

Reflective plenary

7 What do you understand now about writing an effective introduction to your report? Make a list of guidance to use when you write up your Individual Report introduction.

Study skills

It can be helpful to write your introduction quite late in the process of writing and after you have written the main body of your report. This can help frame the report clearly and keep it cohesive.

When you work on your own issue for your Individual Report, you will need to work independently of others.

Discussing causes and consequences

Skills focus

✓ Researching, analysing and evaluating information

✓ Developing and justifying a line of reasoning

✓ Communicating information and reasoning

Objective

- To learn how to set out an analysis of a global issue

How can I discuss causes and consequences in my report?

Starting point

1 Think of an example of a 'cause and effect' relationship. A 'cause and effect' relationship is when one thing causes another thing to happen. Make brief notes and then explain it to a partner.

Explore

In this section, you will learn how to set out your understanding of causes and consequences in depth in your writing. In Global Perspectives, causes and consequences can be complex. Consequences can form a sequence, so that one consequence goes on to cause a second consequence, which may then cause a third consequence, and so on. Effective analysis in Global Perspectives sets out the impacts of global issues. One global issue can have similar and different consequences in different national or local contexts.

Take a look at this example of Sitaram's. Here are some notes that he has made about a cause and its consequences.

Source: Dr Paul Jepson (2020), 'Rewilding: a climate change solution'

Cause: Human hunting in Pleistocene era

↓

Consequence 1: Bison/horse/woolly rhino/mammoth numbers collapse. Some extinct. [short term]

↓

Consequence 2: Herbivores aren't there to eat grass. [consequence then becomes a cause]

↓

Consequence 3: Vegetation changes. Peat. Boggy. [long term]

Here is how he wrote about this in his report.

> Human beings changing ecosystems is nothing new. Human beings moved into the Arctic region in the Pleistocene era. Large herbivores including bison, horses, woolly rhino and mammoths thrived here. 'Unsustainable levels of hunting' had a severe impact – and many creatures were driven to extinction (Jepson 2020). The vegetation in the region today is very different from the grassland that woolly mammoths grazed. If you don't have herbivores nibbling away constantly, different plants take over. Today the region is peaty and boggy.

where the consequences had an impact

the main cause

the short-term consequence

the long-term consequence

Notice how Sitaram has used quotation marks to indicate where words are directly taken from a source.

Here is another section of Sitaram's report. He is discussing the causes and consequences of biodiversity loss at a national scale.

> All of the global causes of ecosystem damage are present in India. Each cause results in specific national and local consequences. Take over-exploitation as an example. *Economic Times* journalists Chandra & Chandra (Oct 2015) explain just how severe over-exploitation was in India under **colonial** rule. Their analysis deserves to be taken seriously. Staff journalists from a widely read business newspaper would not want to risk their publication's reputation for accuracy. They draw on 'personal diaries, memoirs and photos of British officers who ruled India'. These officers believed that 'hunting was good for the development of "character", and that it trained young men to be good soldiers'. As a consequence, 'Between 1875 and 1925, at least 50,000 tigers were slain.' The impact of this over-exploitation is still with us: 'Cheetahs, which once roamed freely, are extinct today. Tigers, rhinos and elephants remain endangered species.' People have been working extremely hard to raise tiger numbers, yet since 1971 they have gone up by only 300. Congress MP Shashi Tharoor's perspective is that India should demand reparations to fix the damage. Chandra & Chandra calculate that the ecosystem would cost £15 billion to turn round. I will develop this idea in the course of action, but it is undeniable that £15bn could go a long way.

where the consequences had an impact

Vocabulary

colonial: colonialism is the practice by which one country directly controls other countries and uses their resources to increase its own power and wealth

the main cause

the short-term consequence

the long-term consequence

Again, notice how Sitaram has included clear references to the authors he is referencing and the date of their research. Quotation marks show where he is including their words directly.

Activity: Summarising causes and consequences

2 Work with a partner. Sitaram has set out a number of causes and consequences in this section. Find one cause and summarise the consequences in a flowchart.

Develop

A good way of organising your thoughts on multiple causes and consequences of an issue is to use a mind map. Here is one of Sitaram's mind maps.

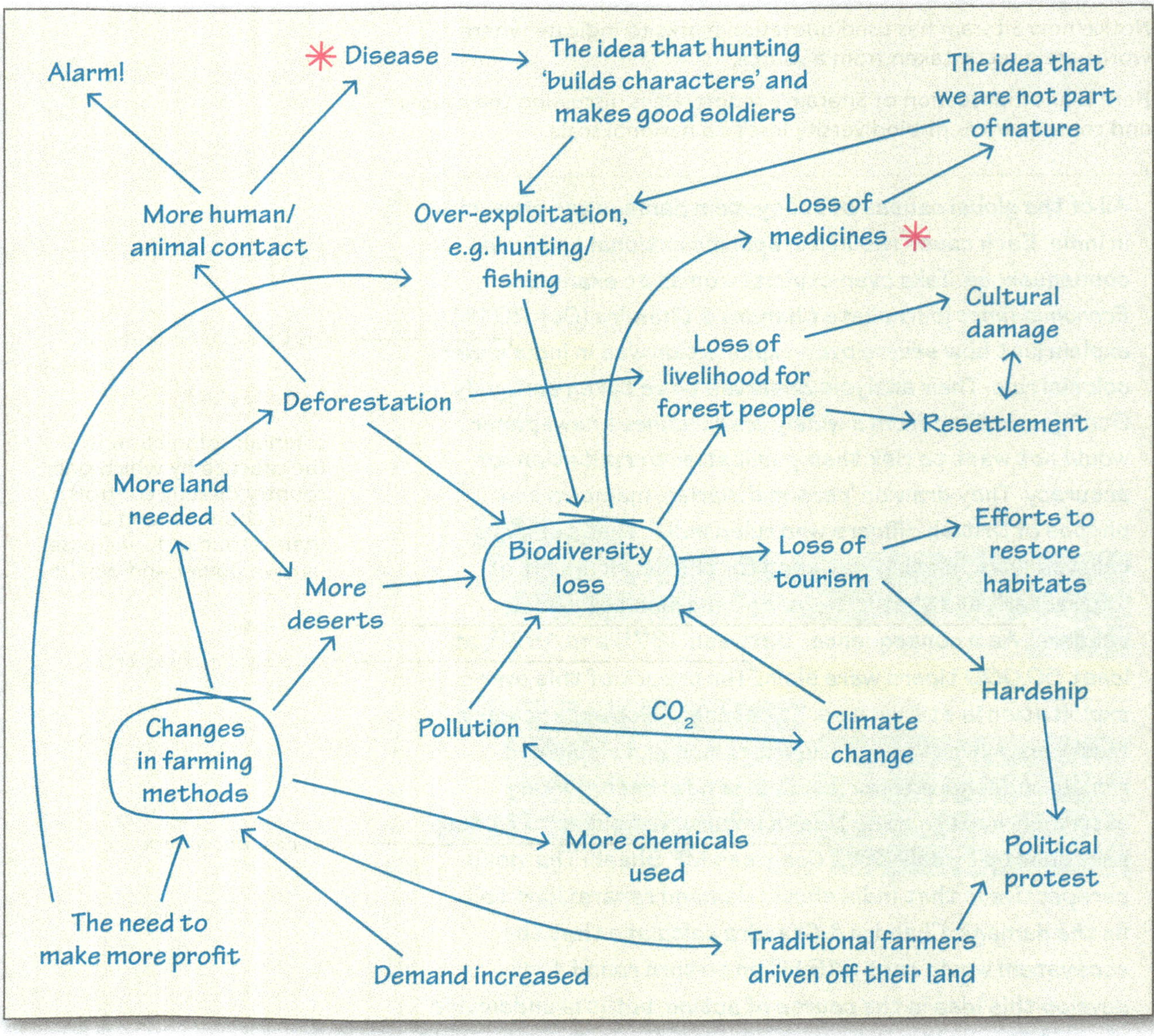

Here are some sentences in which Sitaram identifies one cause and several effects.

> *The need to increase profit margins has driven changes in farming methods. As a consequence, farming globally has become more intensive and uses more chemicals. These chemicals in turn have caused pollution. Global biodiversity has suffered as a result.*

Activity: Explaining causes and consequences of an issue

3 Work with a partner to write similar sentences about the causes and consequences of biodiversity loss. Use Sitaram's mind map, as well as your own prior knowledge and understanding.

Activity: Explaining causes and consequences of an issue in greater depth

4 Work with a small group. Combine your sentences to create a paragraph. Explain how the causes and consequences of this issue are linked.

Apply

Now focus on the issue you have been discussing with your group.

Final task

5 Work together with your small group. Create a mind map to organise your thoughts on how the causes and consequences of your issue are linked.

6 Work with a partner. Write some sentences about your issue. Identify one cause and several effects in each one.

7 Work with a small group. Combine your sentences to create a paragraph. Aim to explain how the causes and consequences of your issue are linked.

8 Now share your paragraph with your teacher.

Study skills

When you work on your own issue for your Individual Report, you will need to work independently of others.

Reflective plenary

9 Complete this sentence.

When explaining the causes and consequences of a global issue in my Individual Report, I will need to...

Selecting perspectives and discussing them in your essay

Skills focus
- ✓ Researching, analysing and evaluating information
- ✓ Developing and justifying a line of reasoning
- ✓ Communicating information and reasoning

Objective
- To select and describe a range of perspectives

How do I know if I have got a good balance of perspectives in my report?

Starting point

1 Think of an issue that you have some knowledge about. Think of someone who has a perspective on that issue. What judgements do they make? What evidence and/or reasoning do they use to convince other people that their judgement is correct?

Explore

In this unit, you will learn how to select perspectives and work them into your discussion in your essay. You will need to make sure that you are doing more than explaining the perspective, and that you are, instead, working it into your discussion and argument.

When you select perspectives to include in your discussion, you will need to make sure you have a good balance. Consider at least one **local** and/or **national perspective** *and* one **global perspective** on your issue.

Sitaram has kept a log of perspectives he has researched. Not all of them will appear in his final piece – but he has made sure that he has researched a range to choose from.

Key terms

local perspective: a viewpoint on a local issue which is supported by reasoning and evidence

national perspective: a viewpoint on a national issue which is supported by reasoning and evidence

global perspective: a viewpoint on a global issue which is supported by reasoning and evidence

Activity: National and local perspectives

2 a Look at the table on the next page. What makes a perspective 'national'? Explain whether it concerns where the author comes from or the impact it has on a country.

b What makes a perspective 'local'?

Vocabulary

indigenous: people who originally lived in a country or region before colonisation

Should we use rewilding to restore damaged ecosystems? (This is the global *issue*)

Who (when/ where)	Judgement (Yes / Mixed feelings / No)	Reasoning	Evidence	Global, national or local perspective?
Shiva (2020)	Yes – but that doesn't mean eating lab food	Real farming is farming with nature, in nature's ways. So, let's rewild farming.	At Navdanya, we grow healthy food by conserving biodiversity	**Global** – farming with nature can save the planet
Jepson (2020)	Yes! 100% It could be a 'global warming game changer'	Nature based solutions work best.	For example, the Arctic. Rewilding = grassland. Grassland keeps greenhouse gases stored.	**Global** – it could be a 'global warming game changer'
Nogués-Bravo (2016)	No – too risky	It is a 'Pandora's box' – consequences are unpredictable.	Some success stories – but some actual harm to ecosystems. Better to use trusted methods.	**Global** – ecosystems across the globe damaged.
Monbiot (cited in Shiva 2020)	Yes – let's eat lab food	Farming causes greenhouse gases. So, let's stop it.	Lab food is already being produced. Will allow us to hand back vast areas of land to nature.	**Global** – greenhouse gases = global impact
Chandra & Chandra (2015)	It will cost money. The former colonisers should pay.	British hunting in India drove creatures to extinction and critical levels. They should pay.	Records prove the damage. Congress MP calls for reparations.	**National** – it is about the impact of biodiversity loss on India
Staff at the Wayanad Wildlife Sanctuary (website)	Yes. Species are restored and indigenous civilians benefit.	Indigenous people depend almost completely on the forest for their livelihood.	The Kattunayakan people are 'experts in the collection of wild honey and wax'.	**Local** – it is about the impact of the issue on local people
People who live in protected areas (quoted in Mongabay 2020)	Have mixed feelings about being resettled	Some people want a new life. Some will miss the old.	Better healthcare education, etc. but the new location is not the same.	**Local** – it is about the impact of the issue on local people

Develop

By way of example, you will now focus on discussing one global perspective and one local perspective on a global issue. You will also look at how to support both with relevant information.

Ms Nambiar has given the class a checklist.

Checklist for success

Make sure:

- each perspective is relevant to the question
- you set out clearly the claims and judgements that are made
- you set out the evidence
- you summarise the evidence and reasoning that backs up each perspective.

Here is Sitaram's discussion of Shiva's **global** perspective.

Another global perspective in favour of rewilding comes from Indian scholar and environmental activist Vandana Shiva. Shiva supports 're-wilding the land, our food and our bodies' (Shiva 2022). For her, 'we are what we eat'. The problems stem from the fact that what we eat has less and less to do with nature. Current farming methods are driven by the need for greater profit. They use a lot of chemicals. They use a lot of energy. This energy and chemical use causes greenhouse gas emissions which in turn drive climate change.
So does that mean that we should stop farming and grow food in factories like Monbiot suggests? Shiva argues that this would be a nightmare. For her the rewilding can actually happen on the farm. She cites work done at Navdanya where they grow organic food that is healthy. Their methods look after the insects that pollinate the crops and the soil. Her vision is of a world where rewilding does restore ecosystems but does not mean throwing farmers out of work.

Here is Sitaram's discussion of a **local** perspective.

People who live in the Wayanad Wildlife Sanctuary have a perspective on the consequences of rewilding. Animal numbers have improved, but for some people this has had a negative impact on their way of life. For example, it can be challenging to walk 17 km to go to school in an area inhabited by wild animals (TOI 2021). The more animal numbers increase, the more contact between animals and people occurs – and this is not always welcome. Many people have applied for resettlement schemes (Mongabay 2020). There have been positive consequences. Many welcome the new homes, healthcare and jobs. Inevitably, some miss their old way of life. This affects older people in particular. We can assess the local perspective on rewilding as being to some extent mixed.

Notice how Sitaram has referenced each perspective with the author's name and the date of their study or publication. Full details will be given in the bibliography. He has used quotation marks to show where he is quoting their work directly.

Activity: Giving feedback

3 Has Sitaram met Ms Nambiar's criteria? Remember, his question is: *Should we use rewilding to restore damaged ecosystems?* Discuss with a partner.

Study skills

When you work on your own issue for your Individual Report, you will need to work independently of others.

Apply

Final task

4 Work with a small group.

Select one of the perspectives you identified earlier as part of your research and discussion. Add notes on this perspective to a table like Sitaram's on page 157.

Who	Judgement	Reasoning	Evidence	Global National Local?

5 Work with a partner. Use the group's notes to draft a paragraph which explains this perspective.

6 Swap your paragraph with another pair. Give each other feedback. How have they explained the perspective successfully? What improvements could they make?

7 Now share your paragraph with your teacher.

Reflective plenary

When you write your Individual Report, you will need to include, as a minimum, one global *and* one local and/or national perspective on the issue.

8 What ideas do you have at this point about the issue that you will research for your independent research project? What perspectives do you think there could be on this issue?

9 Write some guiding notes for yourself to use when you write up the 'perspectives' part of your Individual Report. You could include in these notes an annotated version of the paragraph you wrote with your partner.

Writing about evaluating sources

Skills focus
✓ Researching, analysing and evaluating information
✓ Communicating information and reasoning

Objective
- To evaluate sources in writing

What am I looking for when I evaluate a source?

Starting point

1 Take 60 seconds to note down all the things to consider when evaluating a source. Compare with a partner.

Explore

In this section, you will apply your understanding of how to evaluate sources to those you have identified in your research. You will be able to establish which ones are worth including. You will then learn how to write about these sources in your report.

Sitaram is using this set of questions to evaluate a source:

1) Who wrote this source?
2) Where was it published?
3) When? (Is this recent enough?)
4) Why? (Can you trust their motives?)
5) What is the author's expertise?
6) Is the viewpoint backed up by evidence/reasoning?
7) Why is this information useful? (How does this fit into your overall discussion?)

Here are his answers:

1) Dr Vandana Shiva
2) The website of *The Ecologist*
3) 24th January 2020 – recent enough
4) *The Ecologist* is 'an environmental news and analysis website with a focus on environmental, social and economic justice'. Dr Vandana Shiva is a 'scholar and environmental activist'. They are giving their perspective. They would be concerned with accuracy – otherwise they would be discredited. Shiva wants to argue against Monbiot's case for lab-produced food.
5) She has a doctorate and a long list of published works.
6) She bases her argument on her work at Navdanya foundation working across India.
7) It gives a perspective that is for rewilding but not *against* farming.

Here is a paragraph that Sitaram wrote about another source.

Nogués-Bravo's perspective is that rewilding is not the best strategy. He is quoted in a *Science Daily* report of 2016 saying, 'Scientifically we are in the dark about the consequences.' This is significant. An associate professor who specialises in biodiversity says clearly that he is not convinced that rewilding is the best course of action. The *Science Daily* report explains that others in the scientific community share his perspective. *Science Daily* uses university press releases. These documents can be trusted to represent the universities' perspectives. I have not found evidence that the situation has changed since the report was published. He bases his concerns on 'the lack of critical thinking' done by rewilding projects. He says that scientists need to do more basic research. If we can't predict the effects, then this must be a concern.

Activity: Analysing a source

2 Work with a partner. Identify which part of Sitaram's paragraph answers each of his 1–7 questions above.

1)

2)

3) '2016' and 'I have not found evidence that the situation has changed since the report was published.'

4)

5)

6)

7)

Develop

Activity: Writing an analysis

3 Work with a partner. Write a paragraph about the Shiva source from the Explore section above, using Sitaram's responses to the 'evaluation' questions.

Apply

Final task

4 Work with a partner. Use a source that you have found. This should be relevant to the issue you have been discussing. Answer the seven questions.

5 Work with a partner. Use your answers to the questions in activity 4 and Sitaram's evaluation of Nogués-Bravo's *Science Daily* source to write a paragraph evaluating your source.

6 Now share your paragraph with your teacher.

Study skills

When you work on your own issue for your Individual Report, you will need to work independently of others.

Reflective plenary

7 How would you finish the incomplete sentences below?

When I write up my Individual Report, I will evaluate my sources. When I do this, I will make sure… This is because… In addition, it will be important to… This is because …

Making judgements about perspectives

Skills focus

✓ Developing and justifying a line of reasoning

✓ Communicating information and reasoning

Objective

- To make judgements about different ideas
- To develop your points of evaluation

How should I weigh up the perspectives and come to a judgement for myself?

Starting point

1 Think of a time when you had to make up your mind about who was right. For example, a time when two people gave you contrasting opinions about:

- the best way to do something
- why something happens
- what the right thing to do is.

How did you decide who was right?

Explore

You have already selected and discussed perspectives, as well as evaluated their sources. In this section, you will learn how to make judgements about different ideas for yourself. This will be an important part of your research discussion.

The set of questions in the table on the next page can be used to interrogate the perspectives you are considering in your investigation.

Sitaram is using a set of questions to evaluate his perspectives.

Research question: *Should we use rewilding to restore damaged ecosystems?*

	Perspective 1 Nogués-Bravo	Perspective 2 Monbiot	Perspective 3 Shiva
a How would they answer the question?	No	Yes	Yes
b What course of action do they support?	Tackle climate change & deforestation.	Lab food. Don't farm.	Sustainable farming methods.
c What are the strengths of this perspective?	Makes sense. Introducing large species = unpredictable consequences. Ecosystems complex things.	Technology has achieved great things in past. So future too.	Sustainable methods used successfully in past.
d What are the limitations of this perspective? Are any questions not answered?	How to tackle deforestation and climate change?	What happens to poor farmers?	Can sustainable farming feed cities?
e What is your overall judgement? **1** Highly convinced? **2** Somewhat convinced **3** Neither convinced nor unconvinced **4** Somewhat unconvinced **5** Highly unconvinced Explain your answer.	2) I can accept that if rewilding is unpredictable then we need to be careful. Not fully convinced. Issue urgent. Needs urgent course of action.	4) Convinced that tech could have role. Not convinced about lab food. Farmers will not accept being thrown off land.	2) Sustainable farming must be part of solution. Methods used by foundation work well. Could this work on global scale?

Activity: Making a judgement

2 Do you agree with Sitaram's overall judgements in **e** above? Discuss your assessment with a partner.

Develop

Here is a paragraph that Sitaram has written as part of his research project. In it, he evaluates Nogués-Bravo's perspective.

Nogués-Bravo (2016) is extremely sceptical about rewilding. He does not think this is a valid solution to the issue of species loss. He says the results can be unpredictable. I know that contact between people and wild animals can be a serious issue. Locally, rewilding has not caused ecosystem damage. However, there are cases globally where rewilding has caused damage. I am therefore convinced by this analysis. The course of action that Nogués-Bravo puts forward has two elements: i) more research into rewilding, ii) focusing for now on tackling climate change and deforestation. These courses of action seem sensible. I would like to know more about how he thinks this can be achieved. It is clear that the issue is urgent – but Nogués-Bravo does not give us a clear short-term course of action.

Management of herbivore numbers has caused controversy at the Oostvaardersplassen nature reserve, a rewilding project in the Netherlands.

Activity: Making a judgement

3 Work with a partner.

a How would you describe Sitaram's judgement of Nogués-Bravo's perspective?

- Strongly supportive
- Fairly supportive
- Undecided
- Fairly unsupportive
- Strongly unsupportive

b Give reasons for your answer.

Apply

Final task

Now focus on the issue you have been discussing as a group.

4 a Work in your group. Using a table like the one on page 163, evaluate at least two perspectives on your group's issue. Aim to include local or national and global perspectives on the issue.

b Discuss your answers to questions a)–e) and note your group's answers.

5 Work with a partner. Use your group discussion notes from activity 4 to evaluate a perspective on your issue. Write a paragraph explaining your judgement.

6 Now share your paragraph with your teacher.

Study skills

When you work on your own issue for your Individual Report, you will need to work independently of others.

Reflective plenary

7 How would you complete this sentence?

When I judge perspectives in my Individual Report, I must make sure to…

Reflecting on your developing personal perspective

Skills focus

✓ Reflecting on processes and on own learning
✓ Communicating information and reasoning

Objective

- To learn how to set out a reflection on how your personal perspective has developed

How can I explain how my personal perspective on an issue has developed?

Starting point

1 Think about a time when you changed your mind about something. What was the issue? What was your view or perspective beforehand? How did it change? What caused that change?

Explore

In this unit, you will learn how to set out a reflection on how your personal perspective has developed. A number of factors can influence your developing personal perspective: your exploration of different perspectives; your analysis of causes and consequences; or the research you have conducted into possible courses of action.

Sitaram has drawn a chart that shows how his perspective has developed over the course of his research.

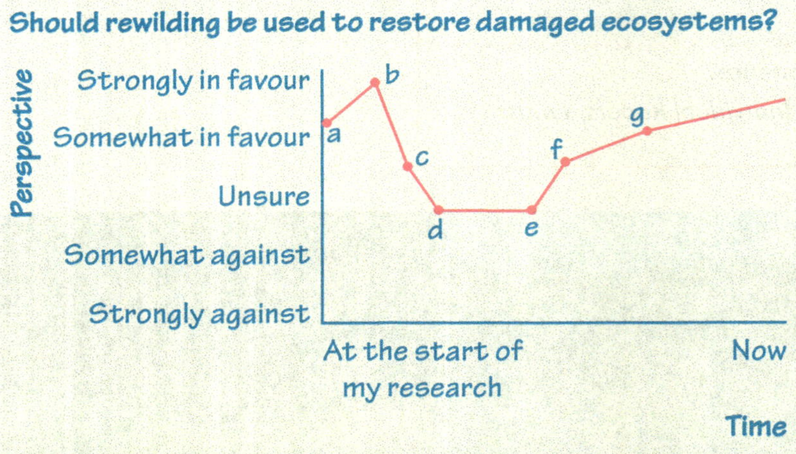

He has identified six factors that influenced his perspective.

Key research and reflection:

a I read about the destruction of wildlife 1875–1925

b I read Jepson and how rewilding could be a 'global warming game changer'

c I read Nogués-Bravo and how we can't be sure of the results

d I read about some local difficulties with wild animals

e I found out about resettlement programmes

f I read Shiva & about 'rewilding farming'

g I reflected on Shiva and a positive course of action

Activity: Developing your personal perspective

2 Discuss this question in pairs: *How would you describe the impact of each piece of research on Sitaram's perspective, as shown by his chart?*

Develop

In this paragraph, Sitaram sets out his reflection on how his perspective has developed.

When I began my research, I understood that biodiversity loss was a serious issue globally. I knew that damaging farming methods was one major cause. I knew that something needed to be done and thought that rewilding seemed like a good idea. I found out more about the scale of the damage caused by hunting nationally during the colonial period (Chandra & Chandra 2015). This confirmed my initial perspective. Getting tiger numbers up by 300 has taken 45 years. When I read Jepson's article (2020), about rewilding the Arctic, that made me even more in favour. It appeared that rewilding would not only bring back magnificent species but also help to stop global warning. Nogués-Bravo (2016) changed my thinking though. Until that point, I had not considered the risks. Local news about wild animal encounters and difficulties with resettlement made me wonder if the risks for people were just too great. The challenging thing was that the term 'rewilding' seemed to mean different things to different people. Shiva's perspective about rewilding farming changed my perspective significantly. I saw that there need not be a conflict between farming and biodiversity. Thinking about the course of action made me more in favour. I saw that sustainable farming methods can be linked to safer food and better justice for the people that work on the land. I also found out about the positive consequences of resettlement if it is conducted properly.

Activity: Developing perspectives

3 In pairs, identify where Sitaram's written reflection matches the graph above.

Study skills

When you work on your own issue for your Individual Report, you will need to work independently of others.

Apply

Final task

4 Look back over your notes on the issue you have been discussing. How has your perspective on your question evolved? Make a chart, then compare it with your group.

5 Work individually. Write a paragraph explaining how your personal perspective has developed on the issue you have been discussing. You may find the highlighted phrases in Sitaram's paragraph useful.

6 Now share your paragraph with your group or your teacher.

Reflective plenary

7 Think about when you do your Individual Report. What good reasons might there be for changing your perspective on an issue? What good reasons might there be for not changing your perspective? Make two lists.

Making a case for a course of action

Skills focus

✓ Researching, analysing and evaluating information
✓ Developing and justifying a line of reasoning
✓ Communicating information and reasoning

Objective

- To learn how to make a case for a course of action

How can I make a case for a course of action effectively?

Starting point

1 Think of a time when you were part of a group of people and you put forward a suggestion about what should be done. What issue were you discussing? How did you try to persuade people that your suggestion was a good idea?

Explore

In this section, you will learn how to set out possible courses of action. You will learn how to explain how a course of action can be implemented. This will involve evaluating how practical your proposal is and its possible impact. You will learn how to justify the course of action you have selected with reference to your analysis of the issue and different perspectives on it.

Sitaram looked again at his mind map which organised his thoughts on the causes and consequences of the issue. He used this to organise his thoughts on how the issue should be resolved.

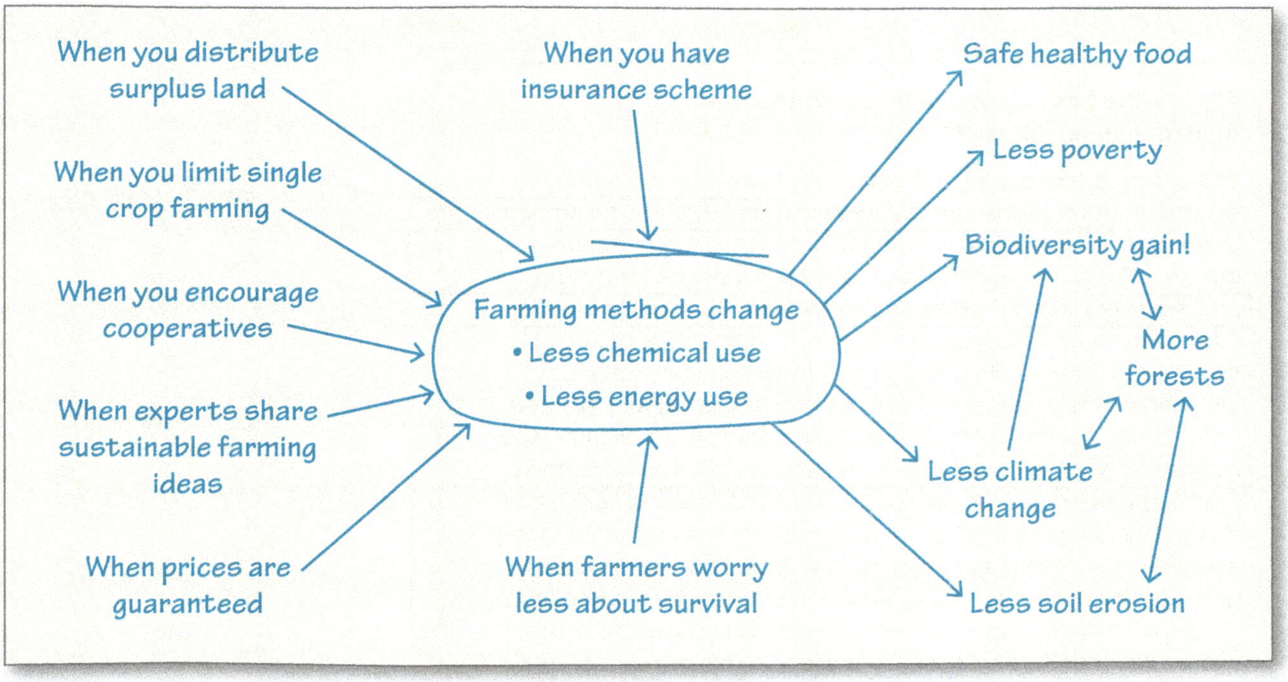

Activity: Causes, consequences and solutions

2 Work in a small group. What cause/consequence relationships has Sitaram mapped out? For example, 'Changes in farming methods will lead to safe and healthy food'.

Develop

Here is Sitaram's draft paragraph which explains courses of action to resolve the issue.

What is the best course of action to restore damaged ecosystems?

There is no single cause for biodiversity loss. That means that we should not look for a single solution. I do not think the answer is lab food. That would give too much power to the companies (Shiva, 2020). I do not think the answer is simply reintroducing species everywhere that they have died out. That would involve taking too many risks (Nogués-Bravo, 2016). A range of actions are needed. Individuals doing simple things can help reverse biodiversity loss. Imagine if every person with a balcony planted a bee-friendly plant in a pot. Urban biodiversity would be improved. Agriculture is a big cause of biodiversity loss. Changing farming methods has to be a big part of the solution. As Shiva (2020) has made clear, farming itself is not the problem; it is corporate, energy and chemical intense farming that is at fault. How do we make farming less corporate? My research has shown that in Kerala, the department of agriculture encourages sustainable farming (Government of Kerala, 2021). To make farming less corporate, farmers can form cooperatives. This makes them less dependent on corporate finance. Communities that own their own land have everything to gain by looking after it for the future. That means they look after the soil and biodiversity can thrive. To make farming less energy intensive, cultivation of traditional varieties of crops should be encouraged. They do not need energy input because they are native to the climate. To make farming less chemical intense we can use insurance schemes. Instead of paying money for insecticides, farmers can take out a policy which will pay out if their crops get damaged. When the insects are left to live, the species that eat them thrive too. Governments globally need to introduce land reform. Land that is not productive should be given to poor farmers without land. Poor farmers that have good land do not cut down forests. When the forests are left alone, the whole ecosystem can recover. This will in turn have a positive impact on climate change and make farming easier – and less damaging to biodiversity.

explains there is not a single solution
rejects a course of action
explains why
how it would address the issue
proposes a course of action
how it would address the issue
proposes a course of action
how it would be implemented
how it would address the issue
proposes a course of action
how it would be implemented
how it would address the issue

Activity: Evaluating a course of action

3 a Work with a partner. Think about how practical these proposals are and about their possible impact. How effectively has Sitaram justified his course of action?

b What aspects of Sitaram's course of action has he supported effectively, with evidence and reasoning?

c Which are you less convinced by? How could he improve his justification?

Apply

Activity: Causes, consequences and solutions of our issue

4 a Work with a partner. Look back at the causes and consequences of your global issue. What courses of action could deal with them? Who would implement a course of action and how? Make some notes.

b Work with a small group and share your thoughts. Develop a mind map together.

Study skills

When you work on your own issue for your Individual Report, you will need to work independently of others.

Final task

5 a Work with a partner. Write a paragraph to explain a course of action that would resolve your issue.

b Swap your paragraph with another pair. Think about how practical their proposals are and their possible impact. How effectively have they justified their course of action? Make notes, then discuss your findings as a group of four.

- What aspects of their course of action are supported effectively with evidence and reasoning?
- Which are you less convinced by? How could they improve their justification?

c Improve your paragraph in the light of feedback from the other pair.

d Now share your paragraph with your teacher.

Reflective plenary

6 Complete this sentence.

When I write the course of action for my Individual Report, I will need to…

Writing a conclusion

What should I put in my conclusion?

Skills focus
- ✓ Researching, analysing and evaluating information
- ✓ Developing and justifying a line of reasoning
- ✓ Communicating information and reasoning

Objective
- To learn how to write a conclusion to a report about a global issue

Starting point

1 When have you had to write a conclusion before? This could be in another subject. What similarities/differences do you think there might be with the conclusion of a Global Perspectives report?

Explore

In this section, you will learn how to write a good conclusion. This is important because a good conclusion is a crucial part of a *cohesive* report.

Ms Nambiar has given Sitaram a few bullet points to help him write his conclusion.

Checklist for success
- ✓ Give yourself sufficient space – around 200 words.
- ✓ Summarise the different perspectives you have explored.
- ✓ What perspectives have you supported?
- ✓ What perspectives have you rejected?
- ✓ Do you need to emphasise any courses of action?
- ✓ What really matters in the end?
- ✓ In summary, how do you answer the question you set yourself?

Here is Sitaram's conclusion.

Rewilding can mean different things to different people. It is hard to give a simple 'yes' or 'no' answer to the question 'Should we use rewilding to restore damaged ecosystems?' Monbiot (cited by Shiva 2021) argues that we should eat food grown in labs. However, that gives too much control to the people that own them. The social cost for farmers would be too great. Nogués-Bravo (2016) says we should not press ahead with rewilding if we don't know the consequences. That has to be a sensible approach. But we can't stand still. Biodiversity loss is far too pressing an issue to simply wait. As Ban Ki Moon has said, 'Saving our planet, lifting people out of poverty, advancing economic growth [...] these are the one and the same fight' (Address to the 66th General Assembly of the UN, 2011). Taking practical action is possible. Shiva (2020) has shown that sustainable farming is effective. It delivers biodiversity and good safe food at the same time. It always helps to have government on your side. Governments need to get to grips with the issue of land reform. If they do, surplus land can be farmed sustainably. Changing farming is one form of rewilding. Protecting forests is another, but the two are linked. The less pressure is put on land by intensive farming, the longer the land can stay productive. In the final analysis, if our food needs are met sustainably, then there is no need to cut down forests. So we can rewild. Our magnificent creatures can then find a home.

Sitaram has highlighted his conclusion in different colours. Each colour matches a bullet point from Ms Nambiar's list. For example:

✓ What perspectives have you rejected? = ☐

Activity: Analysing a conclusion

2 Match the other colours to the bullet points in Ms Nambiar's checklist.

- Summarise the different perspectives you have explored ☐
- What perspectives have you supported? ☐
- Do you need to emphasise any courses of action? ☐
- In summary, how do you answer the question you set yourself? What really matters in the end? ☐

Develop

A conclusion should not introduce new ideas. It should build on the analysis that has been presented.

Activity: Evaluating a conclusion

3 How successful has Sitaram been? Do all of his points build on the previous analysis or has he introduced something new here? Discuss with a partner.

Apply

Activity: Building a conclusion

4 In your group, discuss how you could conclude the analysis of your issue. Use Ms Nambiar's bullet points to help you.

Final task

5 a Work with a partner. Use your notes from activity 4 to write your conclusion.

b Swap your conclusion with another pair. Tell them what they have done well and how they could improve.

c Improve your conclusion in the light of the feedback you have been given.

d Now share your conclusion with your teacher.

Reflective plenary

6 Complete this sentence.

When I come to write the conclusion for my Individual Report, I will need to…

Study skills

When you work on your own issue for your Individual Report, you will need to work independently of others.

Writing a bibliography for your report

Skills focus
✓ Communicating information and reasoning

Objective
- To learn how to organise a bibliography for your report

How should I organise my bibliography?

Starting point

1 What would you expect to find in a bibliography? How would you expect to see one organised? What is a bibliography for? Compare your ideas with a partner.

Explore

In this unit, you will learn how to organise a bibliography for your report.

Ms Nambiar is giving the class some advice about **citation** and **referencing**.

Ms Nambiar

You need to reference whenever you use other people's facts, figures or ideas. Basically, if you use any information that is not widely known and has been researched or written by somebody else – cite it. Not doing this is like thieving. You are taking someone else's research and pretending it is your own. The term for this is plagiarism and it is against our values.

Student

How do we decide what's widely known?

Say if you referred to when a government policy was introduced. That is an example of a widely known fact. You wouldn't need a citation to show where you got that information. If you use someone's perspective from a podcast about the policy, that, on the other hand, would need a citation. Or if you use some facts and figures you found in a newspaper article about how this policy is being implemented. You are using other people's ideas or facts they found. If in doubt – cite it. Everything that you cite, you must also reference in your bibliography. A bibliography is a list at the end of your research paper. Citation is like signposting and happens in your main report.

Key terms

citation: a reference to a specific piece of work in the body of a document

referencing: giving details about a source that you have used, so that somebody reading a work can find the source for themselves

Activity: Understanding when to reference

2 Work with a partner to answer these questions.
   a What do you reference?
   b What do you not need to reference?
   c Why is referencing important?

Develop

Ms Nambiar has produced a checklist for her students.

Checklist for success

✓ Make sure your bibliography is in alphabetical order by the author's surname.

✓ Answer these questions *in this order*:

- What is the author's (or authors') name(s) and initials?
- What is the title?
- Where was the article published? (e.g. in a journal or newspaper)
- When was it published?
- What page was it on? (if in a book or printed journal)
- What date did you access the article?
- Where did you find it? (include a URL if you found it online)

Sitaram has begun compiling his bibliography. Here is his work so far.

Bibliography:

Shiva, V. Rewilding food, rewilding farming. First published in *The Ecologist*, 24 Jan 2020.

Jepson, P. Arctic rewilding could mitigate climate change. First published in *Rewilding Europe*, 17 Feb 2020.

Cell Press. Experts urge extreme caution on 'rewilding' to save wild places. Science Daily. 8 February 2016. Available at: https://www.sciencedaily.com/releases/2016/02/160208134418.htm last accessed 20/05/22

Cronon, W. 'The Trouble with Wilderness; or, Getting Back to the Wrong Nature' in *Uncommon Ground: Rethinking the Human Place in Nature* New York: W. W. Norton & Co., 1995, 69–90.

Government of Kerala. Department of Agriculture Development and Farmers' Welfare Scheme outlay 2021–22 Available at https://keralaagriculture.gov.in/en/schemes/ last accessed 12/05/22

- *organisation* ✓
- *name of specific webpage* ✓
- *link to webpage* ✓
- *Accessed day/month/year* ✓

Prerna Singh Bidra. Resettlement is a voluntary option for families in Wayanad Wildlife Sanctuary 'Mongabay' India Mongabay website. Accessed 20/05/22

Chandra, R. & Chandra, S. (2015). Reparation for destruction of wildlife: That'll be 15 bn Pounds, your highness. *The Economic Times* 12 October 2015

- *author surnames and initials + year* ✓
- *title of article* ✓
- *name of newspaper/magazine* ✓
- *day month year* ✓
- *page numbers missing*

Activity: Checking a bibliography

3 Work with a small group. Study Ms Nambiar's checklist and how she has marked some of Sitaram's entries. (You could also look back at Unit 2.4.3.)

a What has Sitaram done well in his bibliography?

b How could it be improved? What needs to be added?

Make two lists.

Apply

Final task

4 Work with a partner.

a Improve Sitaram's bibliography.

b Compile a bibliography from the resources you have found for your work in this section.

c Now add the correct references in the paragraphs of the report that you have written so far.

Reflective plenary

5 Complete these sentences.

When I set out the bibliography for my Individual Report, I must make sure that I…

I will also need to check citation in…

Check your progress

In this section, together with your partners and your group, you have learned the following:

- I can identify a global issue that I would like to see improved, changed or resolved.
- I can explore some different perspectives about an issue.
- I can research my chosen issue and suggest an action to improve, change or resolve it.

- I can select a global issue of importance which has a range of impacts in the world today.
- I can focus my discussion on an ethical dilemma or causes of conflict, damage, difficulty, or hardship, or simply disagreement.
- I can research a range of different perspectives on the global issue.
- I can focus my report on the perspectives of different people.
- I can propose an appropriate action and suggest how it could be implemented.

- I can engage with different perspectives and demonstrate that I fully understand the arguments, reasoning or claims upon which these perspectives are based.
- I can demonstrate fully and effectively that I understand why different people have different perspectives.
- I can logically and coherently analyse an issue by considering the reasons for conflict or disagreement/causes of problems and the consequences/impacts of the issue.
- I can consider analytically different possible courses of action.
- I can draw logically on my analysis of the issue and set out effectively a single course of action to change, improve or resolve the issue.

Next steps

- You are now ready to work on your own. Choose one of the topics set out in the syllabus and identify something that interests you.
- Conduct some initial research and use it to refine a globally focused question. You can get help from your teacher with this part of the process – but from then on you must work independently.
- Use this question as the title for your report. What are the different impacts in different places or for different people?
- Show that you understand the arguments, reasoning or claims that these perspectives are based on. Show that you understand why different people think in the way that they do. Explain why there is conflict or disagreement about the consequences of your issue. Analyse the causes and consequences in depth.
- Research some different possible courses of action and propose a course of action that you think will change, improve or resolve the issue. Explain why you think it is the most appropriate or effective course.
- Present your report as a structured essay, including a bibliography. Make the most of this opportunity to develop your understanding and set out your considered perspective on the issue.

Section 5: Carrying out a team project

5

An important and rewarding element of your Global Perspectives study is having the opportunity to work in a team. You will have the chance to collaborate on researching different perspectives on a topic of interest to you all and to work together to address a local issue within this topic. This will lead to you deciding on a practical action, followed by a written reflection on what you have achieved and learned.

Although you will be choosing your own topic and issue, this chapter uses as an example the topic 'Sport and recreation', with the team goal of increasing participation in sport or exercise amongst young people. The examples of work in this team project have been written by our authors.

The final two units of the chapter support you to draft a full, written reflection on your learning about the issue your group chose, the action you took to address it, and how you worked together as team – including your own individual contribution to the project.

You will be learning about and developing the following skills:

5.1 Understanding the elements of a team-based project

5.2 Starting your explanation of research and planning

5.3 Honing your research for your project

5.4 Deciding on an action and evidence

5.5 Planning how to evaluate your action

5.6 Collaborating to complete the project

5.7 Planning a reflective response

5.8 Summarising your research

5.9 Writing up your reflections.

Section 5 . Unit 1

Understanding the elements of a team-based project

Skills focus

✓ Collaborating to achieve a common outcome
✓ Researching, analysing and evaluating information
✓ Reflecting on processes and on own learning

Objective

- To reflect on the skills needed to complete a successful team-based project

How do I ensure I am fully prepared to do a team-based project?

This unit will set out the typical requirements of a team-based project so that you are absolutely clear about what you need to do. It will help you and your group decide on an issue to explore.

Starting point

1 You have probably collaborated with other class members and people outside of school on a number of things, such as sports or exercise activities; drama, music or dance performances; jobs outside school; subject-based schoolwork; social activities; charity work or family events. Choose one of these collaborations and note down three key **attributes** you needed to be successful as part of that team.

Vocabulary

attributes: qualities or key features

Explore

Most team projects involve *five key elements*.

- A *group plan* of how your team will research a local issue with the goal of suggesting a solution to this issue. This will take the form of a strategic document that will be added to over time as your plans develop. It sets out what your project hopes to achieve, who will do what and what action your group will complete in support of your project. This team document is called the **Explanation of research and planning**.

- *Collaboration as a team.* This means working together productively to achieve what you want or need to do, sharing responsibilities and working towards a common goal.
- *Working as an individual with your own responsibilities, but in service of the team's goals.* This means demonstrating as an individual how you contribute to the success of the team.
- *Evidence of the action.* The action would be what you did as a team to find a solution to an issue you chose. The evidence might be a photo showing how you organised a charity event, with labels explaining what is happening, or it could be an article in the local press describing your event.
- *Reflective writing.* This is usually an extended report which you complete on your own. In it, you reflect on how effectively your team's action achieved your aims and how the team worked together. You will also reflect on the work you did as an individual and as part of the team, evaluating your own skills and what you learned from the project.

Activity: Evaluating my skills

2 a What team skills do you already have? Rate yourself from 1 (low) to 5 (high). Add any further skills you can think of.

Skill or attribute	My mark
Being a good listener	
Communicating clearly with others	
Contributing positively to discussions with my own ideas and views	
Initiating ideas or approaches	
Supporting or helping others in a team/group	
Taking on roles and responsibility willingly	
Staying focused on the task which has been set	
Sticking to deadlines set by the group (or yourself)	
Being well-organised, both in notes and any other writing	

b Now, discuss your findings in pairs.

- Share examples of when you demonstrated these skills.
- Identify areas you need to work on most, and suggest ways you could do this.

Develop

What would be an effective team project?

Let's look at one example. The team chose the topic of 'Sport and recreation' because four out of the five members enjoy team sports. The other prefers different forms of exercise, such as going on long walks.

In their team, they begin to consider different issues related to sports and recreation. They spend some time looking at newspaper articles. They research different perspectives, and then discuss the topic as a group. Finally, they scribble ideas onto a sheet of A3 paper.

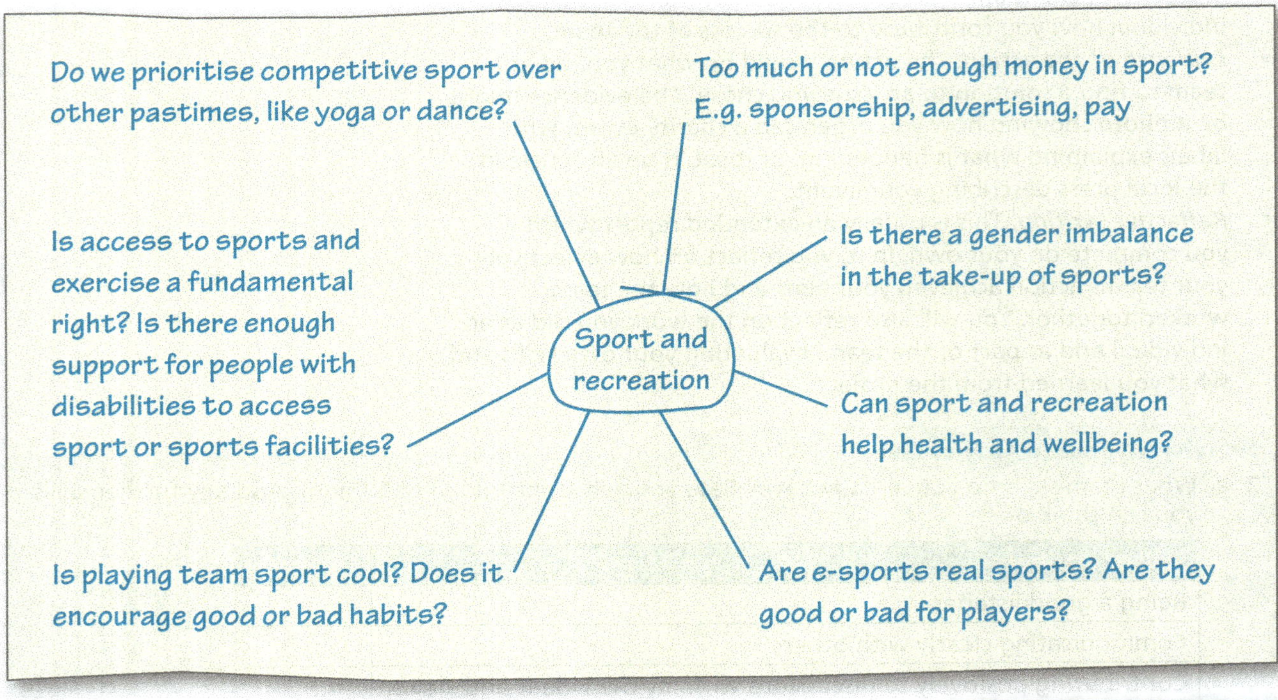

Note how the questions they have added suggest particular perspectives, for example that competitive sport is too dominant.

Activity: Selecting an issue to focus on

3 a What other issues or perspectives could they have added?

b Now, in your own team, begin by identifying a topic from the syllabus that would interest you as a group.

Activity: Researching the issues

4 Although you may already know something about your topic of interest, you will need to research different perspectives to identify an issue and to consider different actions.

a Find recent news stories or blogs related to your topic. You could also do an online image search and see what interesting images it reveals. Talk to others outside your team – parents, teachers, friends – and see what they say.

b What perspectives did you identify through this process? Make some initial notes to get a sense of the range of views.

c Next, in your team, use a sheet of A3 paper to note down as many possible issues or questions around the topic as you can.

The team working on the topic of Sport and recreation have now looked at the different issues and thought about which are relevant to their local situation. Here is an extract from their discussion.

Musa:	Why does everyone assume only competitive sport is good for you? I mean a walk in the countryside is great for relaxation.
Eze:	Yeah – true. Loads of people I know are turned off by team sports, especially girls. I love sports, but I am super competitive!
Yetunde:	Really, Eze? Plenty of girls like team sports! I think we agree sport and exercise is good for you, though, don't we?
Blessing:	Yeah – I guess. Some people need alternatives, but is yoga really a sport?
Maryam:	It's exercise, isn't it? And it can really build strength. So, maybe we look at how we encourage students to take part in sport and exercise, whatever their likes and dislikes?

After this discussion, the team settles on the following issue and aim.

Issue: Widening participation in sport and exercise amongst young people

Aim: In what ways can we encourage students to see the benefits of sport and exercise and participate more?

Apply

Final task

5 a In your team, talk through the issues *you* have identified and narrow your topic down to an issue you can explore and develop locally.

b Write down the overall issue you have settled on and the aim for your project. Make sure you keep your own record of what you have decided.

Remember that the issue you decide on *must* be one that you can successfully research, that presents a range of different perspectives and that can be put into action locally. Check this with your teacher to make sure it is practical.

Reflective plenary

6 The initial work you have done so far could form part of your team **Explanation of research and planning**. Has your team recorded the topic, issue and aim you agreed in the Final task? If not, make sure you do that now. Separately, keep your own log of any thoughts, questions, interests or concerns you have at this point.

Language support

Think carefully about how you word your project's aim. The stated aim needs to make clear that there should be a solution or suggested action that can follow. Questions which help you evaluate and then draw conclusions, such as 'How can/could...?' and 'In what ways...?', are better than descriptive questions such as 'What are...?'

Starting your explanation of research and planning

Skills focus
- ✓ Collaborating to achieve a common outcome
- ✓ Researching, analysing and evaluating information
- ✓ Reflecting on processes and on own learning

Objective
- To understand what an effective project explanation consists of
- To develop your own explanation

How do we effectively plan and explain our project?

The Explanation of research and planning that your team creates together should provide a working, ongoing account of the following:

- the topic and issue you wish to address
- your project's aim
- what each team member will research, and whether this leads to a refinement of the topic/issue
- what roles/responsibilities each team member will have
- the action your team will take to meet the aim of the project
- how you will provide evidence that the action occurred
- how you will measure the success of the action
- what, if anything, changed during the course of the project.

Starting point

1 The case study team in Unit 5.1 chose the issue of participation in sport and exercise because this was something they all enjoyed, apart from one member. Why did you choose your issue? It is useful to agree your **rationale** before you get too far in your research.

Key terms

rationale: explanation of the reasons for choosing or doing something

Explore

The next element of the project to be tackled in the **Explanation of research and planning** is the research your team will do. The case study team have begun to consider who might have a perspective on their issue. Here are the notes they have made, along with some key questions.

Parents – Do they play or have they played sport? What sport/sports? In a team? What was their experience of it? Have they encouraged their children to play sport or exercise? Do they participate in sport or exercise with their children?

Other family members – What is/was their experience of sport, whether team or individual? How do they feel about it? Have they influenced (for good or bad) their siblings?

Students – Do students prefer individual or team sports, or other forms of exercise? What are their attitudes to sport/exercise? Why? What might be the barriers to those who don't take part?
Teachers – What do they feel about sport and fitness both within and outside school? Are the 'right' sports (if any) being taught? How do they encourage non-sporty students to engage with sport? Do they feel the school promotes a healthy culture, including exercise?
Each of the groups above could also be asked how they would increase participation amongst school students.

Activity: Identifying other perspectives

Having a range of further, possibly different perspectives beyond the local environment is good for opening up key ideas and possibilities.

2 Is there anyone else or any organisations who might have a perspective on what could encourage (or discourage) a young person to take part in sport or exercise?

3 What other influences might there be on a student's decision to participate in sport or exercise? You could think about the media, celebrities, fashion and about **access** and **inclusion** for example.

Vocabulary

access: the way into something both literally (e.g. the entrance to a sports centre) and more generally (e.g. the cost of activities or availability of facilities)

inclusion: openness to different people and groups

Activity: Perspectives on your chosen project issue

4 Now, think about the research your team might do.
Who might have a perspective on the topic/issue your team has selected? Discuss and note down possibilities.

Develop

The sports case study team have a clear idea now of what they are investigating. They have expanded their initial discussions and agreed on these areas to research:

- Scientific research into the physical benefits of particular sport/exercise
- Information about emotional wellbeing gained from sport/exercise
- Attitudes towards sport/exercise
- Barriers to participation
- How sport/exercise is managed in schools elsewhere
- How sport/exercise is promoted.

They have also logged their discussions so far and agreed a date to meet, but they haven't agreed roles and responsibilities.

One role worth considering is a chair for meetings. It can be helpful to have someone who will lead the meeting. This does not have to be the same person each time.

The chair needs to demonstrate the following skills:

- able to keep the team on track ("Right, back to what we were discussing...")
- able to stick to deadlines ("We need to finish off this questionnaire before the end of this meeting, so let's get it done.")
- able to involve everyone in the team ("OK, so we've heard your views, Musa. What about you, Yetunde?").

These are skills everyone in the team should have, but sometimes it is useful to have one particular person who has these responsibilities.

Activity: Chairing meetings

5 **a** Who would be the most effective 'chair' in your team? This needn't be the loudest or most confident person!

b Is this something you could do? Why/why not?

The sports case study team are now in a position to partly complete their Explanation of research and planning. This is what they have written as a plan.

Team explanation	
Topic	Sport and recreation
Issue	Widening participation in sport and exercise among young people
Aim and rationale	Because we are all keen on sport, except for one member of the team who is keen to do more, we aim to promote participation in sport and alternative forms of exercise by showing its benefits, such as an improvement in health and wellbeing.
Our research and roles/responsibilities	We plan to research the physical and mental/emotional benefits of particular sports/exercise as well as attitudes to sport/exercise amongst students, teachers, parents, etc. We will investigate how other schools manage sports both locally and globally, and we will also consider how sport can be promoted. Yetunde will chair the team, with Musa to act as **scribe**.

Apply

Final task

6 In your own team, create a similar plan for the first stages of the explanation. Make sure you include the following:

- the topic, issue and aim
- a brief explanation for why you have chosen this particular topic and issue
- any research areas you have identified, although you may feel you need more time to do this
- at least one action for each member of the team (there can be separate roles and responsibilities if you know what different areas you are researching, or it could be a more general fact-finding mission initially)
- any other roles and responsibilities within your team.

Reflective plenary

7 The idea of inclusion may be a key element of the case study team's research, but should it also be a focus for you in terms of how you run your own project?

How can you make sure everyone in your team is involved? Are there any barriers to everyone in the team taking part or contributing?

It is also worth considering how you can make sure you include particular groups in your research. (For example, what might a minority group or people with special educational needs or disabilities think about your issue?)

Continue to keep your own personal log of your answers to these questions.

Key terms

scribe: person chosen to keep a written record; notes key points, ideas and decisions in a meeting, adding who made them

Honing your research

Skills focus

✓ Researching, analysing and evaluating information

✓ Reflecting on processes and on own learning

Objective

- To explore different perspectives on your chosen issue
- To begin to explore possible actions

How can the perspectives we research help us with our aim?

You will need to research local perspectives but also other global or national perspectives which will allow you to gain a greater understanding of the issues. Aim to consider perspectives beyond the most obvious ones.

Starting point

1 Imagine you are part of the case study team exploring sport/ exercise participation. A student in your school mentions that they have been feeling anxious but had heard that taking up yoga might help. Discuss in pairs: what are your first thoughts about yoga being a sport or form of exercise? How could you test whether the student's hope is correct?

Explore

One of the sports case study team members tasked with looking at the benefits of exercise has found an online article from Johns Hopkins Medicine (9 Benefits of Yoga | Johns Hopkins Medicine). This lists nine benefits of yoga, including the following.

www.9Benefitsofyoga ...

5. Yoga relaxes you, to help you sleep better.
Research shows that a consistent bedtime yoga routine can help you get in the right mindset and prepare your body to fall asleep and stay asleep.

> Try It: **Legs-Up-the-Wall Pose**
> *Sit with your left side against a wall, then gently turn left and lift your legs up to rest against the wall, keeping your back on the floor and your sitting bones close to the wall. You can remain in this position for 5 to 15 minutes.*

6. Yoga can mean more energy and brighter moods.
You may feel increased mental and physical energy, a boost in alertness and enthusiasm, and fewer negative feelings after getting into a routine of practicing yoga.

7. Yoga helps you manage stress.
According to the National Institutes of Health, scientific evidence shows that yoga supports stress management, mental health, mindfulness, healthy eating, weight loss and quality sleep.

> Try It: **Corpse Pose (Savasana)**
> *Lie down with your limbs gently stretched out, away from the body, with your palms facing up. Try to clear your mind while breathing deeply. You can hold this pose for 5 to 15 minutes.*

www.9Benefitsofyoga ...

8. Yoga connects you with a supportive community.
Participating in yoga classes can ease loneliness and provide an environment for group healing and support. Even during one-on-one sessions loneliness is reduced as one is acknowledged as a unique individual, being listened to and participating in the creation of a personalized yoga plan.

Activity: Evaluating the source

2 On your own, make notes on the following:

a Can this source be trusted?

b What are its key messages? In what ways does it support the idea that yoga might be beneficial to mental wellbeing?

c What might be an alternative perspective on this?

d In what ways might the information here help you plan your action?

e Has reading this changed your view of yoga? Explain why.

Another case study team member has interviewed students aged 13–16 about their participation in sport and exercise. One 'open' question asked students what they did and did not enjoy. Here are some of the responses:

Student A: In my spare time I'm part of a dance team. We perform at local events. I get such an adrenalin rush from performing in front of an audience, but I also like the social side – having a laugh with friends. It would be cool if we could do dance at school, too.

Student B: I hate all sports. Anything competitive, really. But I do like exercise, especially when I can do it at my own pace. Like my Pilates class – but it's expensive and I can only afford it once a month. I live with a big, noisy family so having time for myself, to relax and get rid of any tension, is great.

Student C: The only exercise I get is walking to and from school each day. I would like to do something, but I'm no good at sport, really, and I worry people will make fun of me if I do an exercise class.

Student D: I love being part of the school swimming team. I feel a sense of pride that I'm representing the school. Our team is quite successful, so I like the feeling of winning, too!

Student E: Lots of sports are just a no-go area for me as I use a wheelchair. There is a local wheelchair basketball team but it's for adults and they don't have a youth set-up. I enjoy practising at the local sports centre but access is very poor – and I don't have anyone to go with.

Student F: I'd really like to try out exercise, but I have a chronic fatigue condition. Everything is too fast and furious, and I can't cope with it. I need something which eases me in.

Activity: Analysis of evidence

3 a What sort of research is this? Is it primary or secondary? Is it **qualitative** or **quantitative**?

b What are the different viewpoints? Does each one give a valid reason worth taking on board?

c As it stands, would these viewpoints lead the team towards any overall conclusions? Explain why.

4 a In terms of planning solutions to their issue, how does this research help?

b Could the school target any of these students to help promote a session to increase participation in sport/exercise? If so, which students?

c Do these responses help you to come up with ideas for a solution (your action)? This could be an activity or some sort of promotional campaign.

Key terms

quantitative: involving or relating to considerations of amount or size; giving figures that can be compared

qualitative: views, ideas, experiences that add quality or depth to a research report

Activity: Logging the research you do

5 Remind yourself of different research methods (for example, primary research such as questionnaires or interviews and secondary research such as reading academic articles – see Unit 2.2.3 and Unit 3.4). Then, in your team, divide up the research you intend to do in order to find a range of different perspectives.

Develop

Look at how the case study team keep a running log of their discussions and findings. This will help them when completing the Explanation of research and planning.

Our team plan
Topic: Sport and recreation
Issue: Widening participation in sport and exercise amongst young people

Days/dates	Notes	Actions
4th meeting Tuesday 6th April	• *Musa and Eze reported back on the research they had conducted. A web article from Johns Hopkins University hospital set out some of the benefits of yoga to mental health and wellbeing.* • *A survey of some school students showed that under 50% took part in school-based sports. Some commented on the lack of suitable exercise-style activities in school.*	• *Find out what would encourage more students to do school sport and, alternatively, whether other activities would be popular if offered.* – *Blessing to research what other schools do.* – *Maryam to follow up on questionnaire.* – *Musa to check out more on physical benefits.* – *Yetunde to talk to Head of PE, Ms Harmer.* • *Next meeting, Tuesday 13th April. Yetunde to chair.*

Activity: Keeping track

6 a What two research methods have the team commented on in their 'Notes' column?

b What broad comments have they made from the research Musa and Eze conducted?

c What evidence is there that the team have assigned different roles to team members?

d What evidence is there that they are addressing a range of perspectives?

Apply

The team now use their log to refine their Explanation of research and planning. Here is the redrafted section on research.

Our research and roles/ responsibilities	Musa will research the physical and Eze the emotional benefits of particular sports/ exercise, while Maryam will look at attitudes to sports/exercise amongst students and parents, etc. Blessing will investigate how other schools manage sports both locally and globally, and also consider how sport can be promoted. Yetunde will chair the team & speak to teachers; Musa to act as scribe.

Final task

7 a Log your team's progress using a planning grid.

b Then, as a team, complete this section of your Explanation of research and planning, setting out roles and responsibilities more clearly.

Reflective plenary

8 What challenges are you encountering? Have you a clear idea of where your project is going, or do you need to refine your ideas? If so, how? Remember to keep your teacher informed. You should also keep your own personal research notes for each source you analyse.

Deciding on an action and evidence

Skills focus
- ✓ Researching, analysing and evaluating information
- ✓ Developing and justifying a line of reasoning
- ✓ Collaborating to achieve a common outcome

Objective
- To decide on a suitable action which will meet the aim of your project

What is a suitable action we can take to meet our aims?

When you work on a team project, you need to decide what action will meet the aim you have set yourselves. In this unit, you will consider a range of actions and how to provide evidence of them.

Starting point

1 A team working on a topic related to sustainability wanted to persuade students to buy fewer new clothes. They organised an after-school workshop in which an older student, who studies textiles, showed students how to make basic repairs or change the appearance of garments (for example, by shortening sleeves). One of the team took 'before' and 'after' photos of the students at sewing machines with their old and refreshed garments.

With a partner, note down:

- what the aim of the project was
- the action
- the evidence (of it taking place and how it worked).

Explore

'Actions' can take many forms. You could, for example:

- produce a video that aims to persuade an audience about an issue
- create and distribute posters or other material educating and persuading people to act or to change their views about something

- organise an event which demonstrates the benefits of something or raises awareness
- lobby someone in authority in order to get them to change their mind about something
- persuade a business organisation to offer something for the good of others.

The action needs to:

- *be something you all agree on*: Make sure the action is one you all agree on and is suitable for the project. It is less likely to succeed if only some of you support the idea.
- *be achievable*: It is no good organising a costly, enormous event that you can't deliver, or something which requires skills beyond the capacity of your team or whoever you involve.
- *match your aim*: Think carefully about whether the action you select will genuinely give you enough evidence to evaluate the success of the project. Where 'persuasion' or 'change' is involved, you will need to know *how* you can tell if things have changed.

The sport case study team have come up with a list of possible actions to increase participation in sport/exercise amongst school students.

- Invite and introduce a motivational speaker – a famous sports star or exercise guru – to talk to the school.
- Organise an after-school 'Try out something new!' session in which students can try yoga, tai chi, an exercise bike or throwing a frisbee.
- Lead a nature walk, using fitness watches to monitor heartbeat, blood pressure, and so on.
- Film a video demonstrating how sport can be inclusive: show students with disabilities or those who are not obviously 'sporty' participating. Or show how classes could be adapted for different levels of experience or energy levels.
- Organise a week-long 'festival of sport and exercise' when the school closes and lots of local clubs and societies run sports and exercise events.
- Design a poster to put up in one classroom to highlight the benefits of doing exercise for physical and mental wellbeing.
- Perform a rap in which each team member takes on the role of someone who likes exercise (for example, a parent rapping about cycling with their children).

Activity: Choosing the action

2 Work in pairs to discuss and write brief answers to the following questions.

a Which of these solutions do you think would be most effective, based on the criteria of achievability and matching the team's aim?

b Explain why. For example, a persuasive poster would be cheap and easy, but may not be effective and it may not be easy to evidence its effect.

Activity: Your action

3 In your own team, you should be in a position to agree what action you could take to meet the aims you have set yourselves.

a Firstly, work on your own to come up with 1–2 ideas for the action.

b Then, join up with your team to discuss the possible actions. You can use a table like the one below to help you decide which to choose.

Possible action	Meets the aims?	Achievable?	Add to short list?
Design and display a poster listing the benefits of doing certain sports and exercise for health/ wellbeing	Yes – if the poster is persuasive and has relevant information. No – will it have the desired impact if it is just a poster? How will we measure its impact?	Yes – relatively easy	Possibly – but may need to add other elements, like a leaflet campaign

Develop

When you complete your action, you will need to provide 'evidence' that demonstrates clearly what was done. Remember that notes based on your research or initial meetings to discuss the project are not suitable as evidence of the action.

Here are two examples of evidence produced by two teams.

Example 1: Sustainability team

The first is evidence of the sustainability action from the Starting point task. The team took a number of photos and included labels.

Language support

When referring to evidence to support your aim, you can use phrases such as 'This *reveals/shows/indicates that...*' or 'This is an *example/ indication* of how...'.

This image shows Mandana making alterations to a blouse which she was going to throw away.

Roya, who studies textiles, showed her how to do it. Roya buys lots of clothes from second-hand shops and upcycles them.

Example 2: Sports team

The sports case study team created a promotional leaflet to advertise their event. Here is the opening part of it.

WANT TO FIND INNER PEACE?

Why don't you join us in going back to nature?

We are offering a dance class on the beach near the school on Thursday 14 May at 4 p.m. for those of you who normally hide away when sports and exercise is mentioned. This mellow, chilled-out dance class will help you to stretch your limbs and ease any aches and pains, both mental and physical. The class will be run by Musa and you can be sure he will play music that will relax and refresh you. Want to take part?

Sign up on the noticeboard by the hall by the end of school on Tuesday. Hope to see you there! Spread the word!

Activity: Relevant evidence

4 How effective are these examples as evidence of the action taken?

a In what way does the evidence link to the aim in both cases (to show how sustainable use of clothes can be achieved; to increase participation in sport/exercise)?

b In what way do they give an effective indication of what happened as part of the action?

Apply

Final task

5 Now complete the next part of your own team's Explanation of research and planning, covering the action you are planning, and suggesting what evidence you might produce to support it. Begin to think of how you could measure its success, too. You could use the following prompts to help you.

Plan of action, Evidence	*We plan to…* *Our evidence will be…* *We want to check we are doing the right thing by…* *We hope this will show that…*

Reflective plenary

6 Talk with other teams and your teacher about your planned action and evidence. It is important that you are flexible, and if better ideas are suggested by what you see (as long as you don't directly copy them), then you should adapt your own proposals accordingly.

Planning how to evaluate your action

Skills focus
- ✓ Researching, analysing and evaluating information
- ✓ Reflecting on processes and on own learning
- ✓ Communicating information and reasoning

Objective
- To reflect on and evaluate the action your team has taken

How do I evaluate our team's action?

When you evaluate something, you make a judgement about it. In the case of your action, you are measuring its success or effectiveness.

Starting point

1 In your team, discuss how you evaluate the success of anything you do.

Explore

Evaluation of your action will depend on what your aim is. If it is to raise awareness or change the way someone feels about something, then it is likely you will need to create **qualitative** follow-up interviews or surveys. However, these things can also be measured **quantitively** – for example, by measuring how many people change the way they act by a later date. For instance, have people bought fewer plastic items two weeks after a team showed them their video on plastic in the oceans?

Activity: Planning your evaluation

2 Talk with your team to make sure you are clear about:

a qualitative and quantitative methods

b primary and secondary research.

3 Are you more likely to use one particular approach than another? Why?

Develop

The sports case study team have added to their Explanation of research and planning so that it also makes clear how they will measure success. Here is their latest draft.

Topic	*Sport and recreation*
Issue	*Widening participation in sport and exercise amongst young people*
Aim and rationale	*Due to our team's interest in sport, except for one member, we aim to promote participation in sport and alternative forms of exercise by showing its benefits, such as an improvement in health and wellbeing.*

Our research and roles	Each team member will explore different perspectives. Umar will look at respected national/global institutions like Johns Hopkins Hospital, USA (Johns Hopkins, 1) and their evidence about yoga's benefits. Musa and Eze will research different aspects of scientific research, e.g. how **endorphins** from exercise can create **euphoria**, but also longer-term benefits (Ripley, 2). Maryam plans to research perspectives from individual students and parents, and Blessing will look at how some international schools have developed a curriculum to support wellbeing. (Star Academy, 3)
Action, evidence and measuring success	We plan to run two after-school activities shown to create positive impacts on health and wellbeing, namely yoga, dance and tai chi. We also plan to show a video from a well-known celebrity promoting exercise. Our evidence will be a video of both events. We want to check we are doing the right thing by giving a questionnaire to participants to measure the percentage who say they will continue doing some form of exercise. We will also conduct interviews on the day to get some instant responses. We hope this will show that our activities have encouraged students to seek out exercise opportunities.

Activity: Understanding the evaluation

4 a In what two ways are the sports case study team intending to measure the success of their action?

b From this information, what sort of evaluation are they using? Is it qualitative, quantitative or both?

5 In your team, discuss what forms of evaluation you might use.

a How could you use some of the same research methods you used earlier in the project?

b What new research methods might you adopt (if any)?

c What form will the follow-up information take? (Will it be gathering data? Looking for trends or specific changes in attitudes?) What will you do to interpret it?

Vocabulary

endorphins: chemicals released by the body to reduce stress or pain

euphoria: feeling of extreme joy

Apply

Final task

Planning for evaluation

6 In your team, update your Explanation of research and planning so it covers the same elements as the exemplar above.

You should now have a clear route-map for your project and action.

Reflective plenary

7 Reflect on the project so far. How effective has your contribution been? Have you suggested ideas? Have you supported the team? What could you improve?

Collaborating to complete the project

Skills focus
✓ Collaborating to achieve a common outcome

Objective
- To learn how to work effectively and collaboratively on your project

How do I collaborate with my team to ensure an effective project outcome?

Starting point

1 What are the collaborative skills you need to demonstrate when working with others? In pairs, list at least six key pieces of guidance for students working in teams.

You should now be in a position to start the detailed work on your project. This unit will take you through what you have done – and what you still need to do.

Explore

By now, your team should have decided on the following:

- the topic and issue
- the aim of the project and the planned action (this may need to be modified in the light of the work you still have to do)
- the evidence for the action
- your individual roles and responsibilities
- how you will measure the success of your action.

Activity: Assessing where you are

2 Check your team's Explanation of research and planning.
   a Are you clear about what you still need to research or do?
   b Do you each have a copy which accurately reflects your decisions and plans?

Develop

You now need to carry out the work to complete the project. In particular, this means planning and carrying out the action.

Activity: Planning and carrying out the action

3 Use this set of questions to help you to plan and carry out the action.

- **a** What does the action consist of?
- **b** Who needs to be approached or informed? Do you need to seek permission from anyone (for example, a teacher or someone outside school)? Who will take on this role of seeking permission? Are there any health/safety aspects you need to discuss or clear with anyone?
- **c** Who is involved in the running of the action itself? Is it all of you – or will one or two of you have specific jobs to do, with the others supporting? Create a list outlining who will do what.
- **d** What people outside your team will be involved (for example, other students, parents or carers, family members, teachers)? If others are involved, what are their roles? Who will inform them as to what they need to do or help with?
- **e** What resources do you need? Do you have to make or create anything? Does a space or location need booking or reserving?
- **f** Does the action have a specific time in which it happens? If so, how is the time split up? What will happen at different times within the slot?
- **g** What information or communication needs to be distributed to those involved? For example, do you need a running order, time schedule, set of instructions for anyone?
- **h** How have you planned for measuring the success of the action? Who is doing what? When and how will you evaluate the responses?

These are just some of the questions you will need to answer as a team in as collaborative a way as possible.

Apply

Final task

4 Create a team 'job' using the questions in activity 3 as a guide. This can be as simple as the template below.

Job to be done	By when?	Whose role?	Notes/follow-up
Speak to teacher about using school hall	Tuesday 7 May	Eze	Hall booked for sports activity for Monday 18 June. Need to make sure yoga mats available.

Reflective plenary

5 At the start, you were asked to consider what collaborative skills you might need to demonstrate. As you planned and prepared for the action, how well did you do the following?

- communicate between each other
- support each other and/or ask for help when needed
- divide up roles and responsibilities fairly and efficiently
- share and develop ideas
- find solutions to problems
- agree deadlines and targets

Planning a reflective response

Skills focus
- ✓ Reflecting on processes and on own learning
- ✓ Communicating information and reasoning

Objective
- To plan your reflective response

How do I create a plan which will make sure my reflections are clear and thoughtful?

It is useful to have a structure for your reflections on your project, so you can organise your ideas clearly. You will also need to cite your sources, so it is important to plan for where these might go in your response.

Starting point

1 When you write essays or reports in other subjects or for other purposes, how do you use headings and/or subheadings? What is their purpose? Discuss with a partner how they work.

Explore

Here is one student's plan for a reflective paper. Read it carefully, thinking about whether this approach, these notes and headings, would work for you.

Brief intro on topic and context 50–75 words • *Quickly sum up topic, issue, aim*
Summary of research findings 225–250 words • *Brief coverage of research done by team; how mine fitted and was used.* • *Different perspectives encountered and considered.* • *Explain what I focused on: my scientific research on endorphin release during exercise; add citation here.* • *How my research and rest of team's research helped towards the action we chose: the activity sessions.*
Reflection on the team project and issue 250–275 words • *How I felt in team discussions – not so good sometimes.* • *How I learned to assert myself.* • *Was supportive to team.* • *Team didn't work.* • *My individual skills as a researcher and in the team – improving my positivity.* • *How I learned that exercise has different physical and emotional responses (add citation); also, how widening definition of exercise can attract 'non-sporty' students.* • *Sum up how my thoughts on sports and participation changed, and what I learned about why people take up sport or exercise.* • *What I could improve about my own performance – e.g. insist on better record-keeping, organisation of team. Push my own ideas forward.*

Evaluating the action 250–275 words
• *Go over actual idea we had – the after-school activities – and why we chose it/how it met our aims.* • *What we hoped to achieve – basically interest in participating more in exercise – mention some of the problems we encountered – like fewer students participating and promoting it.* • *How we used interviews and questionnaires to gauge interest.* • *Need to say something about how this could be improved if we ran this again.*
Conclusion 50–75 words.
• *Overall reflections on the project, and what I got out of it as an individual and team member.*

Activity: Drafting your plan

2 Using the format above, note your own initial ideas on your issue and project.

Develop

Next, begin to add more detailed examples to your initial notes, if you haven't already done so. This will be a useful step towards the final report.

For example, take the bullets that the student hasn't expanded on above. The underlined sections here represent further details:

- *How I felt in team discussion – not so good sometimes: <u>Lacked confidence initially – others dominated.</u>*
- *Learned to assert myself – <u>I put forward my idea for using a promo video, cited evidence of role models in sport (New York Times article – details in my log).</u>*
- *Was supportive – <u>when Blessing was struggling, I prompted her to explain her ideas.</u>*
- *Team didn't work – <u>was badly led – we needed a better chair, didn't have one. Only at end did we start to work in an organised way with a simple agenda.</u>*

Activity: Adding detail to your plan

3 Now add further detail to your own plan. This should include more examples, and you can begin to add in any key sources you are going to reference (like the *New York Times* source above).

Apply

Final task

4 Complete your plan.

Reflective plenary

5 Evaluate how well you think you have covered the core aspects of the reflection in your plan. If need be, refine it by changing or adding to the headings.

Summarising your research

Skills focus
- ✓ Communicating information and reasoning
- ✓ Reflecting on processes and on own learning

Objective
- To effectively summarise the research that you carried out

How do I sum up my research?

Your project report needs to take account of the research you carried out and how it was used or not used as part of the project.

Starting point

1 As a team, sum up as concisely as possible the research you each did. What perspectives were revealed? How did these contribute to your project?

Explore

Read the following response from one student in the sports case study team, summing up his research.

Sample 1: Musa

We looked at Sport and Exercise, and all of us wanted to get more students involved. We all had different things to do and research. Part of our research was looking at the benefits of exercise. I already knew a bit about physical effects so I took that on but it was a bit narrow. Other research was about what made people want or not want to do exercise. We found stuff about emotional wellbeing, too. This seemed really important. This led to our plan to run some after-school activities.

I found and read an article by an elite runner who talked about the buzz he got from endorphin release. I wondered about this and how we could use it in our action. Did exercise need to be very fast-paced to release endorphins? But anyway, this helped me because I knew I felt good after sport but before my research I did not know why. I also wanted to find some proper science reports to back up the article by the runner but I couldn't. I fed back this information to my team but nothing got done about it. They didn't think it was that important.

clearly outlines the chosen topic and project aim

mentions the research done by the team

not really developed or explained

links to the action

refers to personal research he carried out

Activity: Evaluating sample 1

2 There are some issues with this response. Identify where the student:
- refers to key research but does not cite the source
- identifies a problem with developing his research, but does not expand
- identifies his research not being used but doesn't elaborate.

Develop

This student's account lacks detail and is poorly expressed. He isn't able to really say how his – and the team's – research informed the action.

Now read this extract from a second sample. In what ways is her account more successful?

Sample 2: Blessing

Our research explored reasons for the lack of participation in sport and exercise by some students, such as cultural and gender bias, inclusion, aversion to competition, and so on.

While Maryam was doing a feasibility study for how to run multiple-sport activities, and Musa was investigating the physical effects of exercise related to endorphins, I focused on the global perspective – namely, how some international schools approach sport and exercise participation. Through a survey I sent to Malana High School, the data (Report into Malana High School) revealed to me a 30% difference in participation between those who regarded themselves as fit and sporty, and those who saw themselves as either 'unhealthy' or with factors that limited access, such as a chronic health condition or disability. My research directly contributed to our decision to offer an after-school session in which we would run a range of activities with differing levels of physical demand such as tai chi, yoga and dance. Further research showed me that some schools were thinking creatively when it came to exercise and we needn't be limited to conventional activities. For example, one school in Kenya (Bracewell Academy Parent Leaflet) offered table tennis as an alternative to team sports.

details of team contribution to research

writer's own focus

how research was conducted

Activity: Evaluating sample 2

3 Identify how the student:

- uses the research to support a perspective
- cites her own research
- uses the research to inform the action the team implemented
- gives detailed evidence to support further research.

Apply

Final task

4 Draft your own summary of your research.

Reflective plenary

5 What are the main factors that differentiate the quality of the two sample responses?

Writing up your reflections

Skills focus
- ✓ Reflecting on processes and on own learning
- ✓ Researching, analysing and evaluating information
- ✓ Communicating information and reasoning

Objective
- To communicate, in a clear and coherent way, your reflections on your project, including the research done, the action taken and its impact

How do I effectively write about my performance and that of the team?

The remaining part of the reflective paper will focus on the strengths and weaknesses in relation to:

- your own performance within the team
- how the team operated as a whole
- what you learned about the issue you explored
- how successful the action you took was
- overall learning from the project.

Starting point

1 In pairs, discuss how the project worked in terms of the team. Use the collaborative checklist from the Reflective plenary in Unit 5.6 to guide your discussion.

Explore

Read this extract from a report by a member of the sports case study team.

Musa

Reflection on the teamwork, my contribution and the action

Teamwork

In general, our team worked well together. We had regular meetings and took turns to update each other on our research. I realised in the initial meetings that I was dominating a bit too much, so I tried to listen more and encourage others to speak. As someone who loves sport and exercise, I realise I can be a bit competitive and overconfident. As far as the rest of the team were concerned, I think Maryam did a great job organising the activities as a whole; she is very methodical and covered all bases. However, I did point out that we should have considered the needs of students with different abilities. As a team, we had read a report from 'Sports For All', a campaigning body which has tracked how well or badly sports centres and schools cater for students with disabilities, concluding that they were often low on the list of priorities. This was something Maryam was fortunately able to incorporate in the planning for the follow-up activity.

My contribution

In terms of the activities we organised, I led the dance class myself. It was my idea to add dance to the activities as I felt it was important to have an anaerobic exercise as well as more measured, calming ones. They create a different response in the body (Smith 2019) so I wanted to see how students who hadn't done much exercise before responded. The positive response of the students to my class (several asked if we would run further classes) encouraged me that I had done a good job. I felt I contributed strongly by taking such a central role in the activity itself.

Evaluating the action

Throughout the activity, we evaluated participants' engagement and interest in a number of ways in order to assess the success of what we did. Using basic fitness watches, we were able to show participants how their pulse and heartrates fluctuated, but also encouraged them with graphs quantifying the number of steps achieved. We distributed a questionnaire after the first session, asking participants to rate the likelihood they would continue with some form of exercise. The lower-than-expected results led to us reshaping the second session to accommodate a wider variety of activities. Overall, however, I believe we met the aim of the project – to increase participation, even if we were forced to adapt our action as it progressed.

Activity: Reviewing Musa's response.

2 This extract generally works effectively. Identify where Musa has:
- moved clearly from one topic related to the project to another
- provided a detailed account of how the team worked
- been clear about his strengths and weaknesses in relation to his targets
- linked his research to his own contribution
- commented on the improvements the team made as a result of his suggestion
- shown how the team measured the success (or otherwise) of the action.

Develop

The student briefly touches on the issue and what he has learned from it, but this is not covered in any detail here. This would form part of his conclusion. For example, he could add something on:

How he widened his understanding of the different physical effects of different exercises

How he changed his own view of what a 'proper' sport or exercise activity might be

How he reconsidered his attitude to the issue of competitiveness in sport

Activity: Writing a conclusion

3 Use these basic prompts to finish off the report for Musa.

At the beginning of the project, my view about sport and exercise participation was...

Through my research I learned that...

I realised that there were other perspectives on participation such as...

The action we took taught me that...

I now realise that in order to increase participation, we need to be more aware of...

We also need to...

In conclusion, I have learned that...

Apply

Now, consider the core sections of your own reflective paper: the reflection on teamwork, evaluating the action, your own contribution, and your conclusion. You should be able to look at your Explanation of research and planning, any notes you have made, and any planning for the report you did (such as the template plan in Unit 5.7), to help you with content.

Final task

4 Draft the four key sections.

Checklist for success

- ✔ Address the different aspects (teamwork, the action, your contribution, and conclusion) clearly and fully, using separate subheadings if needed.
- ✔ Separate comments on the team as a whole from your own contributions.
- ✔ Identify the strengths and weaknesses in each, and any improvements or changes that were made, or would need to be made in the future.
- ✔ Cite all sources clearly and accurately, ensuring you do not deliberately or inadvertently plagiarise someone else's work or research.
- ✔ Answer the aim of the project – did you and your team achieve what you set out to achieve?

Reflective plenary

5 Once you have drafted the final elements of your report, check it both against the general criteria above, and against the assessment objectives. Identify where it needs improving, and redraft.

Language support

- Use a variety of words or phrases to explain your research: *It revealed/indicated/showed.*
- Link actions to causes or outcomes: *As a result, I/we…*
- Separate things you or your team members did so that it is clear what aspect you are commenting on: *With regard to the final action…*
- Connect ideas fluently and coherently: *<u>This</u> shows how… Initially… later… finally…*

Check your progress

- I understand the elements of a team project.
- I can think of some possible research areas.
- I can make basic notes on a source and what it covers.
- I can identify what makes a good action.
- I can use at least one basic research method.
- I can identify some team skills I do well and some not so well.
- I can create a basic plan for my written reflection.
- I can give a basic explanation of the research I did.
- I can write basic explanations of my performance in the group and what I learned.

- I can generate some ideas of my own for the team project.
- I can generate a range of perspectives and research areas.
- I can note down a range of factors and questions about a source and how relevant it is.
- I can suggest my own ideas for an action my group might take.
- I understand a number of different research methods and can select from them for my own use.
- I can draw on a range of team skills when planning and completing the team project.
- I can create a detailed plan with headings or subheadings, as appropriate.
- I can summarise my research and how it fitted into the team's overall approach.
- I can write a detailed explanation of my performance within the team, and include comments on the action and issue.

- I can select carefully a range of issues and possible aims for the team project.
- I can select a range of perspectives and research areas, and explain why they would be relevant.
- I can evaluate carefully any source I research on the basis of its usefulness and credibility.
- I can suggest a suitable action and possible evidence to support it.
- I understand a wide range of research methods and can choose appropriately to measure success.
- I can use a wide range of team skills and collaborate successfully with my team to produce a plan of action.
- I can create a detailed plan which I can use as a working document when writing my reflection.
- I can summarise my research and that of the team, and reflect on its impact on the project.
- I can write fluently about my performance in the team, what I learned about the issue, and how effective the final action was.

Next steps

- Once you have written a first draft of your reflection, take a copy of it and mark it up with comments on how it meets the criteria set and where more work is needed.
- If you are interested in the issue of widening participation in sport and exercise, do your own survey of sport and leisure facilities locally and keep a record of what sports/exercises they offer, what access is like, and who uses the facilities most.

Glossary of key terms

The terms and definitions in italics have been taken from the Cambridge IGCSE™ Global Perspectives syllabus. Other definitions of key terms have been provided by the authors of this book.

acknowledge: recognise or make clear

action: in Global Perspectives, an action is something the team does to improve or find a solution to a local issue; for example, an action to respond to the issue of loneliness in elderly people in the community might be to set up a rota of visits

active listening: as people are speaking, the team takes their ideas and discusses them further to move the meeting forward

aim: what you are hoping to achieve through a project

analyse: examine in detail to show meaning, identify elements and the relationship between them

annotate: to add notes around a text

***argument:** a series of statements containing reasons and evidence which support a claim about a global issue*

bias: unfairly prejudiced for or against something or someone

bibliography: list of works or sources referred to in the main text (usually comes at the end of the essay)

case study: gives specific information about something or someone and their development over a period of time; case studies are often chosen by researchers because the particular case represents a wider phenomenon

causes: responsible for making something happen

chair: calls meetings and makes sure that the aims of the meeting are met

citation: a reference to a specific piece of work in the body of a document

cite: to refer to

claim: to state or assert that something is true (verb); a statement or assertion about an issue (noun)

cohesion: something that is cohesive consists of parts that fit together well and form a united whole

collaborate: when two or more individuals work together to solve a problem; collaboration is similar to cooperation; most collaboration requires some form of leadership

conclusion: a judgement reached by reflection on arguments, reasoning and evidence

consequences: results or effects of something

context: the context of an idea or event is the general situation that relates to it, and which helps it to be understood

conventions: accepted way of doing things

course of action: an action or solution to an issue or problem

culture: activities such as the arts and philosophy that are important for the development of people's minds

culture²: the beliefs, habits and way of life of a people or a society

describe: state the main points, characteristics and features

economics: the study of the way in which money, industry and trade are organised

economy: money, industry and trade

empathy: the ability to understand and share the feelings, thoughts or perspective of another person

environment: the natural world of land, sea, air, plants and animals

ethics: moral values; the rules and principles that should govern human conduct; when conducting primary research, ethics means research is done with appropriate consideration for those taking part (ethical considerations include seeking the consent of participants, protecting their personal data and making sure they know that they have a right to withdraw)

evaluation: an appraisal of something to determine its worth/effectiveness for purpose

evidence: information about a global issue that helps to develop understanding or prove that something is true or false

explain: say why you think this and support with relevant evidence

fact: something that is known or can be proved to be true

globally: relating to the whole world

global perspective: a viewpoint on a global issue which is supported by reasoning and evidence

interviews: conversations with or questioning of a person

issue: an important subject or problem for discussion

local: relating to a particular area or neighbourhood

local perspective: a viewpoint on a local issue which is supported by reasoning and evidence

log: a written record of ideas or information

national perspective: a viewpoint on a national issue which is supported by reasoning and evidence

objectively: in a way that is not influenced by personal feelings or opinions

observing others: this is a technique in which the researcher observes their subjects in a natural setting, without interfering; it can be a good introductory way of gathering information, but is open to the observer's bias, so needs triangulating

opinion: a view or judgement formed about something, not based on fact or knowledge

paraphrase: when you express what someone says in your own words

personal perspective: an individual's response to an issue after learning, reflection and reasoning

perspective: a viewpoint on an issue based on evidence and reasoning

politics: actions or activities concerned with achieving and using power in a country or society

prediction: what someone thinks will happen in the future

primary research: obtaining information that has not been available before; strategies include interviews and questionnaires – observation is another possibility

qualitative data: views, ideas, experiences that add quality to a research report

quantitative data: involving or relating to considerations of amount or size; giving figures that can be compared

questionnaire: the term used to describe the set of questions you ask an individual

quote: when you include the actual words someone says or writes in your own work

random sample: a sample which gives every member of the sampling frame an equal chance of being selected

rationale: an explanation for a course of action

reasoning: thinking about something in a logical, coherent way

references: citation or quotation of a source of information reproduced in a report

referencing: giving details about a source that you have used, so that somebody reading a work can find the source for themselves

reflection: thinking about or considering something in depth

reliability: the extent to which a research method, experiment, test or measuring procedure will get the same results every time

representative: accurately represents or reflects

research: *the systematic study of a global issue to find evidence and develop understanding*

sample: a number of people chosen from a larger group and used to survey or to provide information about the whole group

scribe: person chosen to keep a written record; notes key points, ideas and decisions in a meeting, adding who made them

secondary research: where you research from sources that already exist – from books, journals or online

secondary sources: information that comes from research already conducted and published by other people

specialist: person with skills that will be useful in a team, e.g. IT skills, artistic skills, ability to speak confidently in public, ability to ask questions

stratified sample: a sample which attempts to reflect the particular characteristics of the research population; the population is divided into strata (age, gender, etc) and the sample is randomly drawn from each stratum

structured interviews: a questionnaire read out by the interviewer who also records the answers

survey: the process of collecting, analysing and interpreting data from a group of people

take minutes: noting the key points that are said in a meeting, especially any decisions made or ideas that are put forward

take turns: when people in a team listen to one person at a time; when another person has their turn, the team listens to that speaker; everyone is expected to speak and to be listened to

technology: scientific knowledge being used for practical purposes

triangulating: using different data collection methods to check that your findings are correct

unreliable: not to be trusted; untrustworthy

unstructured interviews: interview in which there are few, if any, pre-set questions, though researchers usually have certain topics they wish to cover

valid: based on sound reasoning

validity: the extent to which an experiment, survey or test measures what it is supposed to measure

value judgement: an assessment of something as good or bad in terms of someone's standards or priorities

vested interest: a personal reason for involvement in an undertaking or a situation, especially expecting financial or some other gain

viewpoint: someone's viewpoint on an issue is the way that they think about it; for example, they might agree or disagree with something; a viewpoint may or may not be supported by evidence/reasoning

Acknowledgements

Text and figures

We are grateful to the following for permission to reproduce copyright material. In some instances, we have been unable to trace the owners of copyright material, and we would appreciate any information that would enable us to do so.

An extract on p.28 regarding Gabriella D'Cruz, MSc.Biodiversity Conservation and Management, Oxford-Indira Gandhi Graduate Scholar. Reproduced with kind permission; An extract on p.47 adapted from 'Why industrial development matters now more than ever before', and the figure on p.48 'A positive but heterogenous effect of economic growth on poverty reduction (2000–2015)'. Source: https://iap.unido.org/articles/why-industrial-development-matters-now-more-ever, based on first chapter of 'Industrialization as the driver of sustained prosperity' (UNIDO, 2020); Table on p.82 'The Clothing and Textile Industry Today...' The UN Alliance for Sustainable Fashion, https://unfashionalliance.org/. Reproduced with permission; An extract on p.90 from "These facts show how unsustainable the fashion industry is" by Morgan McFall-Johnsen, World Economic Forum, 31/01/2020, https://www.weforum.org/agenda/2020/01/fashion-industry-carbon-unsustainable-environment-pollution/. Reproduced with permission; An extract on p.98 from 'Sustainability Development Goals' 4 Quality Education, Goal 4 targets, copyright © United Nations, 2022, https://www.un.org/sustainabledevelopment/education/ (accessed 16/06/2022). Reprinted with the permission of the United Nations; The Figure on p.98 'Annual GDP growth rates according to four alternative educational attainment distributions' from *Economic Growth in Developing Countries: Education Proves Key*, August 2008, IIASA, Figure 1, https://pure.iiasa.ac.at/id/eprint/17101/. Reproduced with permission; The figure on p.101 'Start with ten impactful actions', from *ACT NOW, The UN Campaign for Individual Action*, copyright © United Nations, 2022, https://www.un.org/actnow (accessed 16/01/2022). Reprinted with the permission of the United Nations; Extracts on pp.144, 153 from 'Reparation for destruction of wildlife: That'll be 15 bn Pounds, your highness' by Raghav Chandra & Shruti Chandra, *The Economic Times, India Times* 12/10/2015, https://economictimes.indiatimes.com/. Reproduced by kind permission of Raghav Chandra; and the definition on p.150 of 'Rewilding' from Collins Dictionary. Reproduced by permission of the HarperCollins Publishers Ltd.

Images

p.7 Rawpixel.com/Shutterstock, p.8 patat/Shutterstock, p.8 aslysun/Shutterstock, p.8 Samuel Borges Photography/Shutterstock, p.8 Tom Wang/Shutterstock, p.9 Prostock-studio/Shutterstock, p.9 Monkey Business Images/Shutterstock, p.10 POP-THAILAND/Shutterstock, p.11 fizkes/Shutterstock, p.14 Prostock-studio/Shutterstock, p.14 insta_photos/Shutterstock, p.14 Rawpixel.com/Shutterstock, p.17 monticello/Shutterstock, p.18 Rich Carey/Shutterstock, p.19 Sipa US / Alamy Stock Photo, p.20 Michael Knitl/Shutterstock, p.22 Ronald Rampsch/Shutterstock, p.23 Adisa/Shutterstock, p.25 AJR_photo/Shutterstock, p.25 Michaelpuche/Shutterstock, p.26 Liza Kras/Shutterstock, p.26 zhuk _ ladybug/Shutterstock, p.27 BearFotos/Shutterstock, p.27 Tatiana Bralnina/Shutterstock, p.29 Joerg Boethling / Alamy Stock Photo, p.31 Riccardo Mayer/Shutterstock, p.32 PI/Shutterstock, p.33 Gonzalo R.J/Shutterstock, p.33 ViDI Studio/Shutterstock, p.35 fokke baarssen/Shutterstock, p.38 Lars Christensen/Shutterstock, p.39 Rocketclips, Inc./Shutterstock, p.39 Gino Santa Maria/Shutterstock, p.41 Neissl/Shutterstock, p.42 photopixel/Shutterstock, p.44 PradeepGaurs/Shutterstock, p.46 Jenson/Shutterstock, p.50 Dmitry Rukhlenko/Shutterstock, p.51 luceluce/Shutterstock, p.54 Nazir Azhari/Shutterstock, p.57 belushi/Shutterstock, p.58 Fernanda_Reyes/Shutterstock, p.58 nakaridore/Shutterstock, p.58 mimagephotography/Shutterstock, p.63 DGLimages/Shutterstock, p.64 James Jiao/Shutterstock, p.66 LStockStudio/Shutterstock, p.64 solar_ek/Shutterstock, p.67 Motortion Films/Shutterstock, p.69 Miera/Shutterstock, p.71 Suradech Prapairat/Shutterstock, p.71 Viktoriia Zolotarova/Shutterstock, p.73 CRS PHOTO/Shutterstock, p.74 Odua Image/Shutterstock, p.75 Prostock-studio/Shutterstock, p.79 Sorbis/Shutterstock, p.80, 81 Baloncici/Shutterstock, p.85 CRS PHOTO/Shutterstock, p.86 Oleksandr Nagaiets/Shutterstock, p.88 Africa Studio/Shutterstock, p.91 Yerbolat Shadrakhov/Shutterstock, p.93 B.Forenius/Shutterstock, p.95 Gorodenkoff/Shutterstock, p.97 CatherineLProd/Shutterstock, p.98 Catherine Grant, Institute of Education Studies, UK, 2017, p.104 GEORGII MIRONOV/Shutterstock, p.106 POP-THAILAND/Shutterstock, p.107 Riccardo Mayer/Shutterstock, p.108 Monkey Business Images/Shutterstock, p.110 tigercat_lpg/Shutterstock, p.111 engineer story/Shutterstock, p.112 Mustafa Ertugral/Shutterstock, p.113 StunningArt/Shutterstock, p.114 Odua Images/Shutterstock, p.115 sunnypicsoz-Geoff Childs/Shutterstock, p.116 Zvonimir Atletic/Shutterstock, p.119 Jenson/Shutterstock, p.120 Oleg_Yakovlev/Shutterstock, p.120 Likoper/Shutterstock, p.123 streetflash/Shutterstock, p.124 Lena 046/Shutterstock, p.124 Prapasri T/Shutterstock, p.128 SpeedKingz/Shutterstock, p.130 Prostock-studio/Shutterstock, p.132 num_skyman/Shutterstock, p.135 Ihsan Iqbal/Shutterstock, p.136 mrealpics/Shutterstock, p.137 Dudarev Mikhail/Shutterstock, p.140 S-F/Shutterstock, p.143 nicolasdecorte/Shutterstock, p.144 Catmando/Shuterstock, p.145 Lakeview Images / Alamy Stock Photo, p.147 SeventyFour/Shutterstock, p.148 mehmetkrc/Shutterstock, p.151 ebin francis/Shutterstock, p.152 Daniel Eskridge/Shutterstock, p.155 kamomeen/Shutterstock, p.156 Jacob Avanzato/Shutterstock, p.159 Sids/Shutterstock, p.160 GIACOMO MORINI/Shutterstock, p.162 haireena/Shutterstock, p.163 Mile 91/C & A Foundation / Alamy Stock Photo, p.164 Original Mostert/Shutterstock, p.165 INTREEGUE Photography/Shutterstock, p.167 clicksabhi/Shutterstock, p.168 Santhosh Varghese/Shutterstock, p.169 DELBO ANDREA/Shutterstock, p.171 Richard Nagle/Shutterstock, p.172 Vinod Pilla/Shutterstock, p.174 Matrix images/Shutterstock, p.174 Olesia Bilkei/Shutterstock, p.175 Andita Photography/Shutterstock, p.177 Sourabh Bharti/Shutterstock, p.179 sirtravelalot/Shutterstock, p.180 Lens Hitam/Shutterstock, p.182 Ververidis Vasilis/Shutterstock, p.183 Mongkolchon Akesin/Shutterstock, p.184 oneinchpunch/Shutterstock, p.186 i_am_zews/Shutterstock, p.188 StockImageFactory.com/Shutterstock, p.189 WESTOCK PRODUCTIONS/Shutterstock, p.192 goodluz/Shutterstock, p.192, 194 MAMIAE T8/Shutterstock, p.193 l i g h t p o e t/Shutterstock, p.193 karelnoppe/Shutterstock, p.195 Image Source Trading Ltd/Shutterstock, p.196 Alba_alioth/Shutterstock, p.198 SeventyFour/Shutterstock, p.200 GaudiLab/Shutterstock, p.201 AnnaStills/Shutterstock, p.202 Anton Vierietin/Shutterstock, p.204 Ebtikar/Shutterstock, p.206 Laboo Studio/Shutterstock, p.206 PeopleImages.com - Yuri A/Shutterstock, p.207 De Visu/Shutterstock.